Fundamentals of School Library Media Management

A How-To-Do-It Manual®

Barbara Stein Martin
and
Marco Zannier

HOW-TO-DO-IT MANUALS®

NUMBER 171

Neal-Schuman Publishers, Inc.

New York   London

Published by Neal-Schuman Publishers, Inc.
100 William St., Suite 2004
New York, NY 10038

Library of Congress Cataloging-in-Publication Data

Martin, Barbara Stein, 1947-
    Fundamentals of school library media management : a how-to-do-it manual / Barbara Stein Martin and Marco Zannier.
        p. cm. — (How-to-do-it manuals ; no. 171)
    Includes bibliographical references and index.
    ISBN 978-1-55570-656-2 (alk. paper)
    1. School libraries—United States—Administration—Handbooks, manuals, etc. 2. Instructional materials centers—United States—Administration—Handbooks, manuals, etc. I. Zannier, Marco, 1972- II. Title.

Z675.S3M27345 2009
025.1'9780973—dc22
                                                        2009007930

Contents

List of Figures

Preface

Although it is still the place where books (and other materials) are organized, housed, and cataloged, the school library media center has become so much more than it was in decades past. At the same time, the role of the school library media specialist has also grown into one of the most exciting careers of the Information Age.

Today's school library media specialist must be knowledgeable about and maintain print, non-print, and electronic resources, both physical items the school owns and electronic ones to which it provides access. In most schools, this professional is also the key copyright specialist and the person who leads teachers in the use of new technologies in learning. He or she is a vital part of the school's instructional team. Being a school librarian means having the right materials, being able to find resources on the Internet, teaching our school community—teachers, students, administrators—how to successfully use information, and being a part of planning and teaching the school's curriculum. The role of school librarian is not really *a* role at all—it is *many* roles. Three of this book's main parts are devoted to one of those main roles.

Fundamentals of School Library Media Management is a guidebook for newcomers to the field. It also offers tips and resources that are of value to those already in the profession as well as to library paraprofessionals and clerks. The book can be read from cover to cover to gain information and help with all aspects of the job, or it can be used as a quick-reference handbook to answer questions and locate tips on a particular topic of immediate need (such as, "I ordered books . . . what do I do when they get here?"). The chapters have information on daily management of the library as well as how to provide the wide range of services needed in a school library. Suggestions are accompanied by diagrams and images that illustrate them as well as by charts, forms, and resource lists and links that can be used as-is to help the librarian stay organized and make his or her job a little easier. The forms and lists offered in this book have all been used effectively on the job by the authors and other librarians.

The book is divided into seven parts. The first part covers the basics; the second through fourth parts cover the three primary roles of a school librarian:

- Library administrator
- Information specialist
- Teacher

The final three parts are a conclusion and look at year-end tasks, selected policy documents, and a directory of sources and suppliers. Details on each part follow.

Part I, "The Basics," is designed to help the school library media specialist get through the year. Topics covered include getting the year started by getting to know the school community and facility, setting goals, getting organized, and communicating with stakeholders.

Part II, "Library Media Specialist as Library Administrator," covers finding and utilizing staff and volunteers, maintaining the budget, circulation, weeding, and inventory.

Part III, "Library Media Specialist as Information Specialist," goes through the steps of selecting, ordering, processing, and arranging books and other materials for the library (including a section on Dewey classification); selecting electronic resources, including databases and Web sites; creating the library's Web page along with using some Web 2.0 technologies; and conducting reference services for students and faculty.

Part IV, "Library Media Specialist as Teacher and Instructional Specialist," is next. The chapters in this section help the librarian become more involved with instruction, from exploring the school's curriculum to collaborating with other educators in the building to enhance learning. Both information literacy instruction and creative library programming are covered.

Part V, "Evaluation," consists of Chapter 20, which gives tips on closing the library for the summer and talks about evaluating the success of the library (and the librarian) at the end of the school year.

Part VI, "Selected Policy Documents," includes the American Library Association's Library Bill of Rights with interpretations and freedom statements as well as sample acceptable use policies.

Finally, Part VII, "Directory of Essential Sources and Suppliers for School Library Media Centers," brings together in one place extensive lists of resources that include book and journal vendors, review sources, audiovisual producers, equipment suppliers, and more. When available, e-mail addresses and URLs are provided to allow for quick electronic access to those resources. Flag, write on, and use this directory of resources as a ready reference throughout the school year, as needed; it will help you save time by directing you to the information you need.

Fundamentals of School Library Media Management is designed to make the many roles of the profession clearer to those entering the field while offering practical tips and organizational tools that will make the managerial tasks associated with the daily administration of the library a little bit easier. Spending less time on administrative tasks will allow the library information specialist to devote more time and resources to participating in and enhancing the education of the library's most important clients—the students.

Acknowledgments

This book is dedicated to the memory of Mrs. Hazel Harvey Peace, a long-time educator and advocate of children's literacy. She was a woman who exemplified character, leadership, scholarship, and service. Her spirit is carried forward and heard through the work of Brenda Sanders-Wise, Bob Ray Sanders, and a very long list of too many people to name. Mrs. Peace is with us in every school and library, every time we read a book to a child, and every time we instruct a child to sit up straight.

The author also wishes to acknowledge the contributions of M. D. (Marjie) Lorica and Mary Hannah Guthrie, with a special thank-you to Herman L. Totten and Robert Sidney Martin. This book is made possible by the perseverance of Charles Harmon, who is the guiding force behind the success of so many meaningful library textbooks.

—Barbara

Thanks to my family and friends for supporting me in my endeavors and encouraging me, especially my loving wife, Katrina, and daughter, Miranda, for being so patient and letting Daddy spend time away from you to work on this book. I am excited and proud that you are working on your degree in library science, Katrina; you are a great addition to this profession. Thanks also to my mother, who instilled in me a love of reading and was happy to spend hard-earned money to buy me books as a child. I am grateful to the UNT SLIS program for the impact it has made and continues to make in my life, with very special thanks to Dr. A. Cleveland, Dr. Stein Martin, Prof. K. Long, and Dr. Totten. Thanks to my partner at work, Christina, whom I learn with and learn from each day on this fun journey to becoming even better librarians, and to my assistant, Sherry, who always smiles and makes the journey a little easier. Thanks also to those who helped me begin or continue on my path of school librarianship, including Holly, Robin, Luis, Karen, Vicki, Linda, Pat, and Hilda.

—Marco

About the Authors

Barbara Stein Martin is the Hazel Harvey Peace professor in the College of Information, Library Science, and Technologies, Department of Library and Information Sciences, University of North Texas. She is director of the school library certification program offered online, with the courses counting as electives toward the ALA accredited master's degree. She has experience as a school librarian at both the elementary and secondary levels in four states. She authored the popular *Running School Library Media Centers* along with several other books and journal articles. She served on the advisory board of the Center for International Scholarship in School Libraries at Rutgers University and serves on the board for the Laura Bush Foundation for America's Libraries, a private foundation providing grants to school libraries. Her husband, Robert Martin, was the first librarian appointed to a four-year term by the president to direct the Institute of Museums and Library Services, a grant-making federal agency supporting museums and libraries of all types. Barbara Martin's goal is to make it possible for any qualified teacher to obtain school library certification and to never again hear a principal say, "We cannot find a qualified librarian for our school library."

Marco Zannier is the lead librarian at Elsik High School in Houston, Texas. He received his bachelor's degree in English from the University of Houston and his master's degree in library and information science from the University of North Texas. He has worked in middle and high school libraries and is a former English teacher at both levels. He is also currently an adjunct professor for the University of North Texas College of Information, Library Science, and Technologies.

The Basics

Smile, and hold your head high! You've joined the proud and elite group of superheroes called "school librarians." Okay, this might be stretching it just a bit, but if you haven't already done so, you will soon realize that you're in a field of hardworking and knowledgeable individuals who perform a wide variety of important tasks in the school. It's a bit daunting, but you're up to the task. You just have to remember that you're qualified, and you must remember the old proverb about the only way to eat an elephant: one bite at a time. Think of this book as a handbook to help you with those little bites. This first part, "The Basics," gets you thinking about the important tasks and issues that you'll need to start working on now so you can set the stage properly. The remainder of the book is divided into parts that represent the three major roles you will have as the school's librarian: library manager, information specialist, and teacher/instructional specialist; within these parts you will find guidance for the many facets of your job as it relates to that particular role. Section V gives suggestions on closing out the school year and evaluating your success.

Although it may go against your nature as a librarian, please use the white space provided on each page to take notes, jot down ideas that pop into your head, or doodle (if you're feeling overwhelmed or just plain giddy). We also encourage you to highlight, draw asterisks and arrows, circle phrases or paragraphs, and underline (don't tell your students this or you'll have all sorts of unwanted problems this year).

Getting to Know Your Work Environment

As a new school library media specialist, there are some things you need to "get to know" before jumping right in and getting your hands dirty. Becoming familiar with the people that you'll be working with and with the library space and the collection will set up a framework in your mind that will help you make decisions about your library, the services you offer, and the librarian you want (or need) to be. All of this will help to create a good working environment.

Knowing the People

No librarian is an island unto himself or herself; if you are the only one giving and receiving in your library, then you are doomed to fail. There are many people with whom you will interact on a daily basis in your job as a school librarian. You have an impact on these people, and they have an impact on you (and your job). Though you are not actually a company and you aren't in the business of making a profit, you should think of these people as stakeholders; they don't officially own shares of your library, but they have an interest in its success. Some may have a financial investment, and others may have invested time, their children, or their future. These stakeholders are givers and receivers, so it is important for you to recognize who they are and how they affect and are affected by your library.

How do you identify stakeholders? Some may be obvious, like the principal and the students in your building. However, there may be people in special relationships with the school and the school library (Communities In Schools members or mentors provided by local large corporations, for example). Talk to people like the former librarian, the school secretary, and veteran teachers—these people are stakeholders and can help you identify others. Record the names and then do a little brainstorming about their relationships with the school library. You might want to create a spreadsheet like the one shown in Figure 1-1. Begin thinking about what your library has done and can do for them—and what they have done and can do for your library. This list or spreadsheet is something you will continue to modify as

Figure 1-1. Stakeholder Identification Sheet			
Stakeholder	Needs	Our library provides:	Our library receives:
School board members			
Administrators (principals)			
Teachers			
Students			
Parents	Resources, activities, learning opportunities	Books, computers with Internet access, story time, research help, seminars and classes	Support, publicity, volunteers, monetary and book donations
Community members			

you add or lose stakeholders and redefine roles and services. Tap into your resources and know your stakeholders' needs; if you meet their needs, they will most likely return the favor.

Knowing the Space

The physical space plays a tremendous role in the library's "feel" or atmosphere, its usefulness, and the message it sends to visitors. You probably had a feeling about your library the first moment you saw it; remember that feeling as you visually scan your library now. Is the library soothing or energized? Does it welcome or turn away? Does it encourage browsing and lounging, or is it saying, "get in, get what you need, and get out!" There are some things you cannot change, like the placement of permanent shelving or windows; however, there is plenty that can be added, modified, or removed to create the feeling you and your school community want and need in the library.

Start by looking at the colors. Is there an overall theme, or does the library look like a box of crayons has exploded? Regional preferences may play a factor in colors, as may school colors. Elementary school libraries are traditionally more colorful than secondary ones, but in all cases it wouldn't hurt to consider the effects of the color scheme. Warm colors like reds and oranges evoke a sense of energy and urgency, whereas cool colors like blues and greens create a feeling of serenity and relaxation. Are there any murals painted in the library? Would a mural (or even hung pictures or posters) help liven up a large, blank wall or brighten a dark corner? Speaking of brightness, look for a moment at the lighting in your library. Natural lighting is comforting and creates a connection with the outside world, but too much of it causes glares and can fade furniture and books. Consider adding a few curtains or shades. If the library has all artificial lighting, it may affect the mood in the library (some types of artificial lighting fill rooms with a sickly yellow glow). If adding windows is not an option, consider counteracting the effect of the artificial lighting with lamps, modification of colors (paint, furniture covers, pillows, rugs, etc.), and addition of murals or paintings to bring a sense of the outdoors into the library.

Now look at the shelving. Is it the appropriate height for your library users? If your shelves are too tall, consider placing books only on the bottom two or three shelves and using the top shelves for display purposes. Also note the placement of the bookshelves in the room. If they are lined up in rows, be sure the spaces between them are ample enough to allow for easy access (consider persons in wheelchairs). If the shelving is along the perimeter wall, consider moving some of the shelving into the open space or adding movable bookshelves in the inner space of the library; they break the monotony and can be used to section off smaller areas for instruction or lounging.

The type of furniture in your library is important to the mood and usefulness of the space. Chairs and tables are necessary for class visits, working on homework, or lounging to read books. Too much furniture, however, clutters the area and interferes with movement. It also makes the library appear smaller than it is. Does the furniture fulfill your students' needs? Take a look at the kind of furniture. Is there a combination of hard furniture (such as wooden tables for working) and soft (such as cushioned chairs for reading)? You're looking for a good mix of comfort and functionality. Look, too, at the placement of furniture within the space. You will need large group instruction areas as well as individual private, quiet areas for leisure reading.

Before you begin moving furniture and creating spaces within the space, you probably want to create a "blueprint" of your library. Figure 1-2 shows a school library's "blueprint" that was created using Microsoft Excel. The drawing becomes useful in planning the layout: you can move the furniture on the drawing and play with the layout without suffering a backache, and it comes in handy as a diagram of the regular layout of the library in case furniture needs to be moved temporarily during the school year (when you're experiencing one of those moments of, "I have no idea where this table goes . . . and wasn't there a beanbag here?").

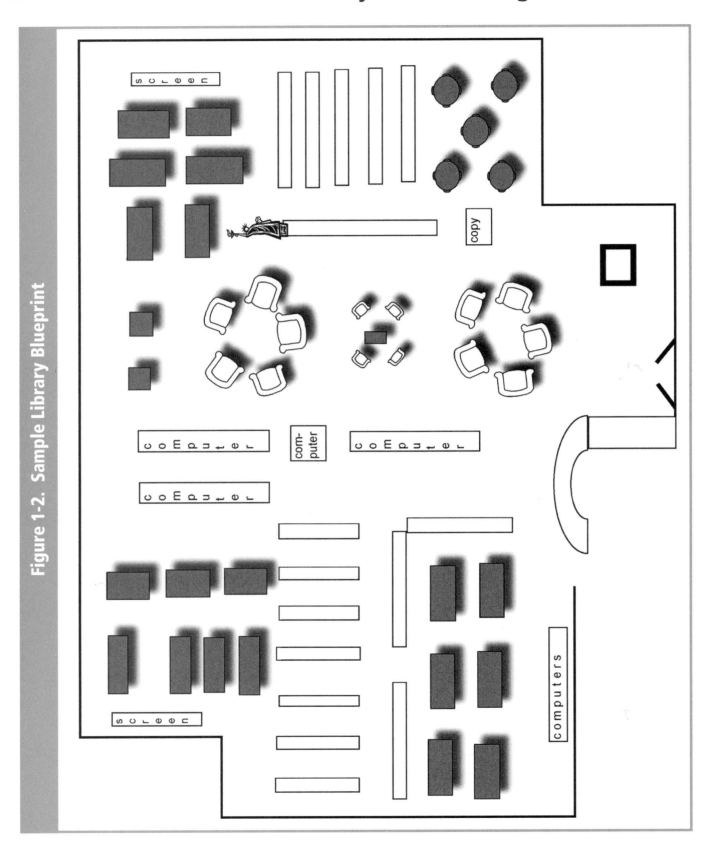

Knowing the Collection

In addition to its atmosphere and staff, a library is most identified by its collection—the "stuff" you have for people to use. Having a high-quality collection of resources that are useful to your school community is essential to having a successfully utilized library. It is important that you know exactly what you are offering to your library users if you want to do a good job "selling" your product. Knowing the collection also makes it easier for you to get rid of old and useless materials and buy newer ones that are in demand. Weeding and ordering are discussed in more detail in Part II.

The first thing you might want to do is get a collection analysis for your library's holdings. A collection analysis can give you data on the age of resources in your collection, topical gaps, weak areas, and much more. Some companies offer this service at a cost, and they will most often provide training and assist you with the process. Book-vending companies, such as Follett Library Resources and Bound to Stay Bound Books, offer a similar service for free to their customers, with added features related to book purchasing, such as notifying you of duplicates in an order and suggesting titles to strengthen the collection.

A collection analysis is a valuable tool, but it must be used with other tasks in mind. For example, you must now also become familiar with the school curriculum because it affects your collection. If your seventh grade science teachers have a long unit that culminates in a project on "The Elements" and you have only one reference book on the subject, it is highly likely that your seventh grade science teachers don't use the library very much, and that the research part of the project is taking place somewhere other than the library, which *should* be the research center of the school. On the flip side, the library could have 35 books about famous Supreme Court cases that are collecting dust because this topic is not part of the social studies curriculum at your school. This is not to say that the library's collection should contain books only about what is being taught in the classrooms; the collection should be diverse and contain a wide variety of subjects that appeal to a variety of users. However, the school library must support the curriculum of the school by providing resources to supplement textbooks and other materials used in the classrooms. How do you find out what is being taught? Meet with department chairs or content specialists, attend team or content area planning meetings, and take a look at the curriculum guides that drive what is being taught (many school districts are now placing their curriculum guides online). Familiarity with the school's curriculum will come with time, so you might want to start by just asking for the main topics in each grade level or subject area. A broad overview of the key concepts will help you begin analyzing the collection for curricular support.

Another important consideration when analyzing the collection is student interest. An elementary school library may have trouble keeping the shelves stocked with books about dinosaurs, whereas they may hardly ever circulate in a high school library. Similarly, high school libraries need plenty of books about colleges and financial aid, while elementary libraries would be wasting money investing in books on those topics. Interests will be quite varied among the school community, but you will begin to notice some patterns in their use of the collection. Keep an eye out for those patterns so that you can tailor the collection to meet the needs of those who use the library's resources.

After you've amassed the perfect collection (which will never truly happen), you will need to "sell" it if you want it to be used. Knowing the collection is the first step.

Setting Goals

When you were offered the job as school librarian, you were probably on an adrenaline high and had trouble sleeping as you thought about all of the exciting things you wanted to do once you started the job. As reality settled in and the first day of school approached too quickly, you may have realized that you might need some help in determining all of the activities and duties that you will need to handle and how to prioritize them. You are new to this field and to your school's library, so you will need some guidance in the form of written goals and objectives to keep you focused and on task for the next ten months. Setting goals will give you a tool to guide purchases, plan programming, and maintain sanity. Once you set your goals for the year, you will want to determine the objectives and priorities for each goal. Setting goals now will help you stay on track throughout the year and will provide you with the means to evaluate your success at the end of the school year.

Use a Goal-setting Form

You might want to start with some sort of graphic organizer that you are accustomed to. Figure 2-1 offers a goal-setting form that can be used for both planning and as a final, official document that you can keep on file and submit to your supervisors. Note, however, that some schools and districts might already have official forms in place for annual goal-setting, so you should check with school administration to see if these forms already exist. Submission of a formal list of goals and objectives to your school administration (required or not) alerts administration about your plans for the library and will help you to receive support throughout the year.

Before you start filling in the blanks in the form in Figure 2-1 (or any form provided by the school), here's a word of advice: make your goals realistic. This does not imply that you should "set the bar low." It's important that you not dream up all sorts of lofty projects that you have no chance of completing, so make sure you have in place a few main, achievable goals so that you don't set yourself up for failure. The "great ideas" that pop into your head can still be done as you discover the time and resources for them,

Figure 2-1. Goal-setting Form	
Librarian:	
Campus:	
GOALS FOR THE 20____ –20_____ SCHOOL YEAR	
Goal 1:	Strategy 1:
	Strategy 2:
	Strategy 3:
Goal 2:	Strategy 1:
	Strategy 2:
	Strategy 3:
Goal 3:	Strategy 1:
	Strategy 2:
	Strategy 3:
Special Project:	Timeframe:
	Expense:
Special Project:	Timeframe:
	Expense:
Special Project:	Timeframe:
	Expense:

but your official goals for the year should help you focus on the big picture of having a successful school library program and a well-oiled library machine.

Three Main First-year Goals

For this first year, there are a few areas you should focus on as you develop or fine-tune a useful school library. They are areas you will work on every year, but they will be especially important this first year as you get to know your library and your school community. Suggested goals for this year revolve around three main issues: improving the collection, collaborating regularly with other educators in the school, and increasing the use of the library and its resources. Those broad goals (in your own words and tailored to fit your setting and ideas) would be listed separately in the left column of the goal-setting form in Figure 2-1. These broad goals should be based on the goals, policies, and overall philosophy of the school district. This information will be available from your school administration.

EXAMPLE: FIRST-YEAR GOALS AND STRATEGIES	
Goal 1 (example): Improve the nonfiction section of the library to attract readers and increase circulation of those materials.	Strategy 1: Add more current biographies and remove outdated ones, esp. non-current celebrities.
	Strategy 2: Increase materials in graphic novel/cartoon/drawing section (741.5).
	Strategy 3: Create a themed monthly display (such as "The Weird and Wacky") to highlight interesting nonfiction books.
Goal 2 (example): Collaborate with teachers to plan and/or implement at least 10 units/lessons by the end of the academic year.	Strategy 1: Attend at least one content area meeting per month to find out what curriculum is being covered; offer suggestions or materials when applicable.
	Strategy 2: Host a cookie social in the library during which teachers are invited to peruse the materials that cover their content/curriculum, and interact with teachers to find out what they need and how you can further work with them to extend/enhance classroom instruction.
	Strategy 3: Promote collaboration and any collaborative projects done by writing an article about it in the school newsletter and library newsletter; post a flyer in the lounge and workroom promoting collaboration.

Since the goals you write are the overarching ideas that drive the decisions and plans you make for this school year, the next step is to develop the specific strategies you will use to accomplish those goals. For example, one strategy that could be used for improving the collection is to run a current collection analysis in order to find outdated items (by date of publication) that will be considered for removal from the collection. A strategy that could help with collaboration might be to meet with grade-level or content teams on a bimonthly or monthly basis. Make sure your strategies are doable; bringing the entire print collection up to date within the past two years based on date of publication, for example, is probably an unrealistic strategy because it would require massive disposal of current holdings and a mammoth replacement budget.

Adding Your Special Projects

After completing the three goals and their accompanying strategies, it's time to write down a few of those great ideas you had. Choose and list a few special projects you'd like to work on this year outside of the three main goals. These special projects might start with phrases such as "Start a..." or "Create...". These are projects you would love to complete and have already begun planning in your head. You may not get to work on all of these; you may start some and then have to relist them next year as "ongoing"; however, they are projects that you think are important and would love to see become a reality. For example, you might want to promote more leisure reading by creating a cozy reading corner with comfortable lighting and furniture for lounging. You are not limited to these projects and can take on or create other projects as the year progresses, but try to think of two or three now that you can have in writing so that you keep them in mind over the next few months.

EXAMPLE: SPECIAL PROJECT PLANS	
Special Project: Create a game area (board games, game table).	Timeframe: 1-2 months (complete by October)
	Expense: Approximately $379 (12 games @ $15 + game table @ $199)
Special Project: Improve layout to allow for "classroom areas" and to create a leisure reading corner.	Timeframe: Complete by December (will require moving of heavy shelves by district maintenance personnel - need to schedule)
	Expense: Approximately $100 (for comfortable chairs or beanbags)

Some Final Goal-setting Advice

Do not rush through your goal setting. You will need to think through your goals and projects, and you might want to do some research in order to determine how much time and money you will need to complete them. Try not to overestimate what you can accomplish in a year—some projects will, of necessity, take more than one year to accomplish. Having your goals and projects planned and listed helps you manage and allot personnel, time, and resources appropriately. If you have a limited budget, this needs to be factored into your goal setting. Doing some research now can help you later if you need to draw up a proposal for additional funding to complete your goals.

Getting Organized and Managing Time

Setting goals is a way to set a course for the year ahead. Now that you've determined the course, it's time to look at some day-to-day tasks that will either keep you on that course or will deter you from it. Organization and time management are crucial to a successful year as the school's librarian. Since you have only just begun this journey, you can do a little work "up front" to prevent you from becoming disorganized or overwhelmed. You have so many different roles and tasks associated with being a school librarian, and your stakeholders expect so much from you, that you must remain vigilant about managing your space, your "tools," and your time. Each person has his or her own way of staying organized (although some claim organization where there is none), so it will be best to tailor your organization methods at work to fit your personality and needs. This chapter offers some proven methods for maintaining order.

Your Office Space

The first step you might consider is organizing your space. If you are in a brand new library, you will be organizing it for the first time. If your library is not new, chances are the previous librarian did not have the same exact organizational style or vision that you have. Where will your desk be located? Some librarians have an office that is a separate room within the library, and some have offices or desk areas located within the general library space. Depending on which physical layout your library has, decide where you need your space to be. Some librarians bring their desk area out of an enclosed office in order to be out in the general library area, and others use creative placement of bookshelves to create an office space where none existed. If your desk area is in the space you want it to be, then sit at it for a short time and determine whether you need to turn it to face doors, user service areas, or windows in order to give you a better view of what is going on. If you will need wall space for posting a calendar or phone list (or inspirational posters reminding you not to stress out), then decide this now and move your desk accordingly. Will you need a filing cabinet beside your desk?

What about a bookshelf? The area you choose and furnish will be one to which you can retreat when you have paperwork to get done, reports to read, or important phone calls to make; try to anticipate now what will work best for you. Your office space will be a completely personal decision based on your knowledge of your own work habits: do you need a quiet and isolated space to get away when there is paperwork to be done, or do you function better surrounded by noise and movement? Of course, there will be limitations to where you can place your area based on such factors as network ports, phone hookups, and electrical outlets. Taking everything into account, you should be able to look around at this point and figure out where you think you might be most comfortable.

Your Work Area

The next physical organization you need to review and possibly change is the "circ area versus work area." This refers to differentiating the space where you circulate materials and interact with students and other library users from the one in which you do the "dirty work" behind the scenes. If your library space can accommodate it, these two areas should be separate. The area for circulation and library user interaction is in the public space of the library and should contain equipment and materials necessary for performing those tasks. The equipment and materials you need for book processing and repair and storing equipment and supplies should, if possible, be located in a place away from the general circulation area. Keeping those items in a separate place helps avoid a cluttered look and contributes to the relaxed atmosphere of the library that students and faculty find comforting (as opposed to the feelings of chaos and frenzy that they might experience walking up to the circulation desk if you have to stop fighting with a book tape dispenser and shove materials out of the way just to give them space to put down their books for checkout). Having a separate area for noncirculation work also gives you countertop or tabletop space for working and spreading out all of the materials you need in order to do that work without filling your circulation area with extra equipment and supplies. Librarians do a great deal of work, but it is best if much of this work takes place behind the scenes so that library users feel you are available for them when they need you and happy to help them; when students think they are bothering you, they will not bother.

Files and Records

Now that you have decided the layout for your office area and your work area, it is time to put into effect a few organizational tricks to keep these areas neat and useful. You are going to learn more than you can imagine during this first year as a school librarian, and unless you are fortunate enough to be a cyborg equipped with artificial intelligence and a large memory capacity, you will need a way to record and store information that will be useful to you in the months and years to come. The first step to doing this is to create files for storing information. Some files will be paper and some electronic. Here are a few suggestions for files that you can create now so you have a place to deposit items later:

- School info: a copy of the calendar for this year, a map of the school, the bell schedule, a list of grade-level or content team members, the student handbook, etc.

- To order/requests: lists of items you need or want, such as furniture, supplies, electronic equipment, software, electronic resources, or print materials; also in this folder keep requests for books made by faculty and students and a list of books you want to place on your next book order.

- Vendors: lists of vendors, business cards with contact information, a list of logins and passwords for sites you use for placing orders, and a list of logins and passwords for electronic resources that you purchase.

- Information for faculty: information you have given or will give to the faculty, which might be a sheet you created about copyright, a pamphlet explaining how teachers can utilize a database, or an article you read regarding the importance of reading aloud to children at school.

- Meeting notes: campus leadership meetings or district librarian meetings, for example.

- Collaboration: notes or forms you've filled in during planning sessions with teams or individual teachers, also handouts, lesson plans, and activity or project sheets that you've created.

- Library printouts: don't re-create printouts you use every year—store in this file items like sign-in sheets, contest entry forms, and original copies of bookmarks that you've created.

- Library reports: circulation printouts, monthly usage reports that you'll create, inventory reports, and your annual goals, for example.

- How-to: instructions you seem to forget, like how to print certain reports in the circulation system, how to change the outgoing greeting on your office phone, how to add a network printer to a computer, or how to fix the computer when a student has "accidentally" hit a combination of keys that makes the display on the monitor appear upside down (yes, it can be done).

Some of these files will work best as electronic files, or perhaps as both a paper and an electronic version, since some of the items such as printouts or e-mails will be in an electronic format to begin with. Always remember to store your electronic files on the network if possible and on more than just your office computer, like on a flash drive or on your home computer as well.

In addition to files, you should probably create a binder just for budgetary records. If you've never been in control of a budget before, you may initially be overwhelmed by the complexity of the budget. Keeping organized records will make the task much more manageable. First, get a copy of your budget and how it is broken down so that you know how much money you are working with; your school secretary probably has this information for you.

Find out if separate budget codes exist for different types of items, like books versus periodicals versus general supplies. If the items have separate codes, create tabs in your notebook for each one so that you can keep purchase records separated by type. If you have an activity account (if you collect fine payments, for example), create a tab for it so that you can track deposits and expenditures. If you will be in charge of creating your own purchase orders, find this out now and get instructions on how to do so. Type out those instructions and place them in the front of the binder. Also place in the binder a few copies of any forms you may need, like deposit or reimbursement forms, just so you have them on hand.

Now create a place for storing other print materials to which you might need to refer throughout the year. Some of those materials are vendor catalogs, professional magazines, the faculty handbook, and phone books. A bookshelf next to your desk is the perfect place for keeping these items orderly and within reach. If you can locate a few magazine files (they are available from any library supply vendor), these will work perfectly for keeping the catalogs and professional magazines tidy on the shelf (be sure to label the files). The magazine files can also be used to keep the print materials upright on your desktop or on top of your filing cabinet if you don't have a bookshelf in your office. A word of caution: weed out these print materials periodically. You don't want to end up with 50 catalogs you never use, 10 copies of the same catalog, and every phone book from the past 5 years.

Library Time

Okay, time to manage, well, time. Your work space looks organized and ready for action, and you are excited about getting to work. One of the biggest enemies of librarians is time. There just does not seem to be enough of it to do everything you want to do for your school community, maintain your status of "expert of everything," save the world, and get home in time to feed the family and tuck in the kids. If you create some ways now to manage your time later, you won't find yourself permanently three days behind.

The first time issue you need to organize is how your library will be scheduled. This might be determined already by your administrator, or it might be something you can influence or even decide yourself. Having control over the management of your own time and the availability of your library's resources so they are most beneficial to all library users is in the best interest of everyone in your school; however, sometimes these things are beyond your control, which is not to say that you cannot propose otherwise. Following are the types of scheduling most commonly used in school libraries:

- Flexible: The school community uses the library when they need it. This type of scheduling makes the resources and the librarian available at point-of-need and promotes and allows for more collaborative planning and teaching. Flexible scheduling is recommended for grades 2 and up as it allows the librarian to provide resources, instruction, and expertise to enhance classroom teaching.

- Fixed: Classes visit on a regular schedule. This type of scheduling works well with early elementary grades (Pre-K–1) as it promotes reading and regular use of the library and helps with return of materials. Fixed scheduling is not recommended for higher grades; it takes away some of the time you could be spending working with teachers and students to enhance instruction and support the curriculum. Some schools have placed the library "in the block" or "in the rotation," which means classes convene in the library as they would for an elective course, and often the librarian is stuck being the supervisor because it is a "free period" for the teacher. Discourage this type of scheduling wholeheartedly as it devalues the library program and your role as an instructional specialist—you should be planning and teaching across the curriculum and by the teachers' sides rather than acting as a babysitter all day. However, the reality is that you will constantly be asked to monitor classrooms of students by yourself during scheduled library time, so you should be prepared to handle these situations.

- Semifixed: This is a combination of fixed and flexible. It is used in some schools to allow the youngest students to visit regularly for book circulation and story time while making the library and the librarian available during the remainder of the time for individual use, instruction, research, and teacher collaboration.

During the time that students are in the library, it is your job to make sure it is a place where all students are able to study and work effectively. As a school media specialist, you will be called on to act as a disciplinarian—just

	Monday	Tuesday	Wednesday	Thursday	Friday
EXAMPLE OF A FIXED SCHEDULE					
8:10 – 8:35	Luster – 2nd	Lopez – 2nd	Lollar – 4th	C. Smith – 2nd	Flores – 2nd
8:40 – 9:05	Powe – 2nd	Veliz – 2nd	Linderman – 4th	Nguyen – 2nd	Cato – 3rd
9:10 – 9:35	Moody – 3rd	Torres – 3rd	Vega – 4th	Rodgers – PreK	Costello – 3rd
9:45 – 10:10	Rogers – 3rd	Holloway – 3rd	Ibarra – 3rd	Martinez – PreK	Tellez – 3rd
10:15 – 10:40	Thomas – 1st	Johnson – 1st	Lugo – 1st	Bermudez – 1st	Valenzuela – 3rd
10:45 – 11:10		Graessle – 1st	Rochin – 1st	Bubeck – 1st	Ngo – 1st
11:15 – 12:15	Lunch; students visit individually on pass				
12:20 – 12:45		Grisbee – K	Gonzalez – K	Marsh – K	Content Team mtg.
12:50 – 1:15	Baker – 4th	Juarez – K	Marin – K	Rodrigues – K	
1:25 – 1:50	Adams – 4th	Goldberg – K	Pre-K PM	Duran – K	
1:55 – 2:20	Kennedy – 4th	Kidd – K	Moore – 3		

EXAMPLE OF A FLEXIBLE SCHEDULE					
	Monday	**Tuesday**	**Wednesday**	**Thursday**	**Friday**
8:00 – 8:30	Garza's class: database demo	Guzman's class: stock market rsrch.	Principal's round table	Fisher's class: YA books + classics	Instructional Specialist mtg.
8:30 – 9:00		Guzman's class: stock market rsrch.	Principal's round table	Flavin's class: YA books + classics	
9:00 – 9:30	Doak's class: biographies	Guzman's class: stock market rsrch.		Fisher's class: YA books + classics	Eng III Team planning mtg
9:30 – 10:00		Guzman's class: stock market rsrch.		Flavin's class: YA books + classics	
10:00 – 10:30	Newman's class: research on STDs	Eype's class rsrch: influential leaders	Eype's class rsrch: influential leaders	Fisher's class: YA books + classics	Joshua's class: fashion research
10:30 – 11:00	Newman's class: research on STDs	Eype's class rsrch: influential leaders	Eype's class rsrch: influential leaders	Flavin's class: YA books + classics	Joshua's class: fashion research
11:00 – 11:30	Newman's class: research on STDs			Fisher's class: YA books + classics	Joshua's class: fashion research
11:30 – 12:00	Newman's class: research on STDs			Flavin's class: YA books + classics	Joshua's class: fashion research
12:00 – 12:30	Davidson's class: literary criticism	Eype's class rsrch: influential leaders	Eype's class rsrch: influential leaders		Joshua's class: fashion research
12:30 – 1:00	Davidson's class: literary criticism	Eype's class rsrch: influential leaders	Eype's class rsrch: influential leaders		Turner's class: book checkout
1:00 – 1:30		Eype's class rsrch: influential leaders	Eype's class rsrch: influential leaders	Fisher's class: YA books + classics	LeGrand's class: French biogr.
1:30 – 2:00	Matthews's class: book checkout	Eype's class rsrch: influential leaders	Eype's class rsrch: influential leaders	Flavin's class: YA books + classics	Turner's class: book checkout
2:00 – 2:30	McCook's class: book checkout	Jackson's class: booktalks	Math tutorials		LeGrand's class: French biogr.

as any teacher must keep order in the classroom, you must maintain order and control in the library. It's your job to know school rules and regulations and to enforce them. Your administration and teachers will be able to provide you with more information.

There is research and rhetoric on every side of the library scheduling argument. Proponents of fixed scheduling indicate the benefits of interacting with all students on a regular basis. They believe flexible schedules allow only a portion of the student population to be reached, which means many students never get the benefit of research skills instruction. Proponents of flexible scheduling believe fixed schedules keep the LMC so busy with regularly scheduled lessons and story times that he or she is not able to devote any time to deeper and more meaningful collaboration and instruction.

Teachers often see the fixed library visit as a chance to dump students and get a much-needed break, so the LMC is not viewed as a valuable colleague for instructional collaboration. The lessons taught by the LMC in a fixed schedule are important, but they lose their value because they are often short, isolated snippets rather than a part or extension of classroom instruction. Flexible scheduling allows the LMC to leave the library to meet with teachers, to co-teach a lesson in a classroom, to work with a class in the computer lab, and to attend or host a team meeting—all activities that allow the LMC to collaborate with teachers to incorporate information skills into classroom instruction and activities. No longer "the story lady," the LMC is seen as an instructional specialist who has the time and resources to help teachers enhance instruction and engage learners.

If a principal is adamant about classes visiting regularly, propose a semi-fixed schedule that includes fixed visits only for certain classes (pre-K and K, for example) or for certain times (only Monday through Wednesday, or only once or twice per month), with the rest of the schedule left flexible to allow for collaborative efforts. Flexible scheduling, however, is preferred and should be proposed and promoted so that students and teachers can truly benefit from the expertise of the LMC.

Whichever type of scheduling you have, you will need a way to keep it organized. Create or purchase a calendar that you can use to schedule classes. Even if you are on a flexible schedule—and hopefully you are—you will need a way to keep track of classes that are coming in for a three-day research project or a collaborative two-day lesson on the importance of evaluating Web sites.

One final suggestion on scheduling your library: if you can get your technology coordinator to set up an electronic calendar that is posted online, you can schedule classes in a place where all faculty members can see the calendar and make requests for library time accordingly. Imagine how easy it would be for you to schedule a class if a teacher e-mailed you saying, "I see you're open after lunch on Thursday and Friday; would you please schedule my classes for those days?"

Your Time

Scheduling your time is as important as scheduling the library. You are the person who can help connect students to books, work with teachers to design engaging lessons and projects, and assist everyone on campus with using good research practices for informational needs. You won't be able to accomplish any of these things if you find yourself constantly swamped and out of time. There are tasks you must perform on a regular basis and meetings you must attend, but because librarians are drawn to people in need of assistance and are always willing to help, they often find themselves plagued with the dreaded "drop everything and do" mentality. Although this practice offers a high level of service because you immediately attend to people's needs as they are brought to your attention, it also will cause you to have a frustratingly long list of incomplete tasks and a collection of tasks you forgot to do because you were busy doing something for someone else. It is not an accident that the acronym for this practice spells out DEAD, because that is how you will feel after running around all day completing tasks as they are thrown at you. Scheduling your time will keep you on track and help you avoid burnout. It has other benefits. It offers a concrete visual you can refer to when deciding whether to accept additional duties or projects, it serves as a way for you (and your supervisor) to see how your time is spent (and how little you really have), and it provides a way for your assistant to help you schedule meetings and appointments if that is part of his or her job.

So—paper or electronic calendar? A paper calendar can reside on your desk for your assistant to modify if this is appropriate, and it is not subject to computer crashes; however, paper calendars are not private and can get messy when modified. An electronic calendar can be changed easily, can be set to notify you of tasks and appointments before they occur, and appointments and calendar events can also be shared with others. Electronic calendars may be subject to electronic damage or erasure, so they should reside in a safe place. With the ubiquity of school networks that include e-mail and electronic calendars that are easy to use, have beneficial features, and allow shared access, an electronic calendar is recommended.

Once you have your calendar set up, *use it*. It is a great organizational tool if it is utilized (see Figure 3-1). Input all events that you already know about, like meeting dates for the year, conference dates, and days that the school is closed. Add tasks you need to complete on a regular basis, like printing out monthly reports or making a monthly newsletter. As you take on additional tasks, set up meetings, and realize you need to complete paperwork or make phone calls, add those items. If there are tasks that you always wish you would remember to do because they need to get done, schedule them. When colleagues ask if you can take on a project for them or your supervisor asks if you can record today's assembly, refer to your calendar. If you can shift and reschedule items, you can accept. If you can't, *say no*. It is easier to say no when you can refer to your calendar and say, "I'm sorry but I'm completely booked today; however, Wednesday and Thursday are light and I would be glad to do this for you then." You will not truly realize how much or how little time you can devote to new projects unless you can see what other commitments you have.

The calendar software used to create Figure 3-1 allows the user of the calendar to share the calendar, create tasks that are linked to the calendar, set reminders or "alarms" that will alert the user of upcoming appointments, and send appointments to other staff members' calendars via e-mail.

Figure 3-1. Electronic Calendar

Calendar					October 2007 - November 2007
Monday	**Tuesday**	**Wednesday**	**Thursday**	**Friday**	**Sat/Sun**
October 15 10:00am Meet w/ Roberto 2:30pm TAKS training	16	17 9:00am Lib. Mtg. (ASF Lab) 11:00am Outlook for Librarian 1:00pm Hilda A+ mtg.	18 12:00pm Pick up lunch for au 1:00pm 1:00 Author Visit 2:30pm SMART mtg (SLIB) 2:30pm send e-mail to Hilda	19 Techmanski's class - poetry	20 21
22 C. Garcia's class: citations how-to 1:00pm Novus Training	23 9:00am Meeting with vendo	24 Annenberg mtg. @ UH	25 8:00am contact Ebsco 11:00am English Dept. mtg. 1:30pm Set up equipment	26 Chavis's class: note-taking 2:00pm Meet Matt re: budg	27 7:30am S.A.T. proctor 28
29 Candy contest 8:00am videoconference 10:30am Meeting w/ Lucas 2:30pm Faculty mtg.	30 7:30am Meet w/ Christina 9:00am Science Dept. mtg. 12:30pm Planning w/ Ngo	31 8:30am Brkfst w/ Sherry 1:00pm Martin: Read-aloud	November 1 Ramiller's class: mood and tone 10:30am Do monthly report 2:30pm Wrkshp: L4U trainin	2 10:30am Soc. Stud. Mtg. 12:30pm Work on portfolio	3 4 Daylight Savings Time Ends
5 9:30am Walk-through with I 2:30pm Smart mtg. (N211)	6 8:30am Meet w/ Stark 11:00am Meet w/ Norm 1:00pm Call Vicki re: worksh	7 8:00am Lib. mtg (Blue Willov 1:00pm Math dept. mtg.	8 Tice's class: databases for research 7:30am set up lite-pro & scr 1:30pm Journey Back in Tim	9 8:00am E-mail Mariella re: p	10 11
12 9:00am Leadership mtg. 12:30pm Art dept. mtg.	13 presentations for Ana's class	14 8:30am Barnes's class: rsrch 12:00pm Meet w/ Ed G.	15 8:00am E-mail B. Stein 11:00am Demonstration: CSI 2:30pm credit recovery (onl	16 8:00am Set up area 2 for pr 9:00am Place order for elec 11:00am Call Pat 1:30pm Contact Miranda re	17 18

Communicating with Stakeholders

Communication from the library is vital because it is a form of publicity and allows the librarian to form and strengthen relationships with library users and stakeholders. This chapter is short, but it offers suggestions for positive communication with your school library community.

E-mail

E-mail is a fast and effective way to communicate with staff and supervisors. E-mail is often used to send overdue notices to students and faculty. It is also effective for interacting with jobbers and vendors, asking questions of other librarians, and contacting authors or storytellers. Here are a few very basic tips for e-mail "netiquette":

- Check your spelling to avoid embarrassing typos.
- Be brief and to the point.
- Do not use ALL CAPS or **bold** print throughout—it will "sound" as if you are yelling.
- Avoid sarcasm—remember, e-mail allows no body language or facial cues to clarify your words.
- If you are making several points, consider a bulleted list rather than lengthy paragraphs.
- You might want to create an automatic signature that includes your name, job title, campus, e-mail address, phone extension, and fax number.
- When replying, include the original e-mail for reference.
- Beware of accidentally sending e-mails to everyone in a mailing list or accidentally replying to all; it is a common mistake that can cause embarrassment, so always review the "To" line before hitting the "Send" button.

IN THIS CHAPTER:
- ✔ E-mail
- ✔ Newsletters
- ✔ Web Site
- ✔ Reports
- ✔ Pamphlets
- ✔ Phone and In-person Communication

Newsletters

Seriously consider publishing a regular newsletter. It can be in print or electronic format, and it can be sent to just the staff or posted online for anyone to access, as in Figure 4-1. Online is recommended because of publicity and storage space. Plenty of software is available to make newsletter creation easy, but you should use what you know, or what the school makes available to you. Whatever you use to create it, your newsletter can do a great job of putting your library in the spotlight and letting others know what's going on and what's to come. Here are a few tips:

- Create a newsletter right away as a way to introduce yourself to the staff and talk about some of the changes you have planned, procedures, and exciting projects.
- Report everything that is and will be happening, but don't be too wordy.
- Use the newsletter to announce contests, author visits, and other special happenings as well as to forewarn the school community of schedule changes, dates when the library will be closed, circulation limitations, remodeling, etc.
- Write articles rather than a giant paragraph.
- Include "fun stuff" like a funny story or comic (keep in mind copyright), a book recommendation, a "library user of the month" award with photo, etc.
- Include links to Web sites your school community would find useful or fun; you can correlate them to the curriculum, the season, holidays, upcoming school events, a recent local or international news story, etc.
- If you aren't artistically inclined, don't worry about it. Use pre-made graphics and layouts, or ask someone to assist you with that part, such as an art teacher or an artistically gifted student.
- If you aren't confident in your writing style or mechanics, get someone on board to help, such as an English teacher or the yearbook editor.

One last word of advice: make the newsletter available to your stakeholders. Get copies (or a link to the published electronic version) to your teachers, your administrators, your district supervisor or coordinator, your superintendent and school board, volunteers, and anyone else you want to make aware of the great things going on in your library.

Web Site

One of the best means of communicating your policies, procedures, library hours, checkout periods, etc., is via a library Web page. Consider having a blog, also. Most schools now have their own Web site and the library, along with all of the teachers, have their own page on the Web site. This is a great

Figure 4-1. School Library Newsletter

ELSIK HS LIBRARIES

BOOKMARK

APRIL/MAY - 2007

MR. ZANNIER AND MS. STARK

HIGHLIGHTS 2006-2007

As we close out our first school year as Elsik librarians, we look back at some of the things we're most proud of from this past year:

- Hosting 3 guest authors
- Brown bag lunches
- Book clubs
- Virtual chat
- "The Oasis"
- Awarding 4 scholarships worth $1500 each

SOME GREAT INTERNET RESOURCES:

Since you won't be doing much teaching this summer, here are some websites you might find handy for your summer fun:

- Family Fun in Houston
- FREE Summer Movies!
- GREAT recipes
- Gardening tips and more
- Summer Safety Tips

LIBRARY CALENDAR

Important library dates:

May 4—All books are due

May 7 though 11 — open as usual, but no book checkout

May 14 — Closed to whole classes; individual students may come on pass

May 14 on — Libraries begin summer preparations, so service is limited

May 21 — Staff members should turn in all materials so records are cleared

May 31—Last work day for the library staff

MORE AUTHOR VISITS

We are very exited about the 07-08 school year and being able to continue with author visits for our high school book clubs. Looking ahead we will have our first visit on September 25, from the award winning author Chris Crutcher. His novels are enjoyed by both students and adults. If you're looking for some summer reading, this is a great place to start. Pick up one of his titles and enjoy.

LOOKING AHEAD

We look forward to summer vacation and a chance for us to reflect on what we've done and what we still want to do. Some library plans for 07-08:

- Look into acquiring some more databases to beef up our electronic research collection
- More book talks in classes and on announcements to promote reading
- Developing a teen advisory board
- Continue programming events to draw students into the library and keep them interested
- Even more involvement with instructional planning and continue working with teachers on lesson design and implementation
- Add "artifacts" to South Library (more info to come)

BOOK SPOTLIGHT: FICTION

Life As We Knew It

By Susan Beth Pfeffer

The story is told through the journals of Miranda, a high school sophomore, and her struggle to hold on to hope after a meteor collides with the moon, putting it off its axis and changing life as it was once known for her and her family.

BOOK CLUB BONANZA

On April 25th our visiting author Teri Lesene, a Sam Houston professor and former Alief teacher, shared the newest and best summer reads in young adult literature with book club members. The culminating event provided students the opportunity to see and hear about the newest books while giving them a chance to win some, along with other door prizes, graciously donated by Follett Books. They also enjoyed a catered meal by Chick-fil-A.

BOOK SPOTLIGHT: NON-FICTION

The Complete Book of Dreams

By Julia and Derek Parker

Explains how and why we dream and includes a lengthy dream "dictionary" divided by themes. Fun, fascinating, and easy-to-read. Illustrated.

way to announce major new activities, new purchases, and more. Software is available for easy Web site creation. You should be the Webmaster, but if you need help, don't hesitate to ask the school's technology specialist or computer teacher. Creating a library Web page is also a task that can be assigned to library staff or volunteers who have this particular skill. See Chapter 6 for more information about staff and volunteers, and Chapter 14 for more information about creating and maintaining the library Web site.

Reports

There are certain reports you may be required to submit to your supervisor or administrator, such as circulation statistics, database usage statistics, and budgetary reports. These reports give specific information that supervisors are looking for in regard to your library; however, they also give only a limited picture of what is occurring in the library. If one does not currently exist for you to use (ask your district library coordinator or the previous librarian), it is recommended that you create a monthly snapshot report for sharing with your supervisors many of the important services you and your library provide for the school community. A sample monthly report can be seen in Figure 4-2. This type of report will let you show not only circulation and purchases but also important nonmanagerial services like collaboration and special programming. Some things you might want to consider including in your monthly report are the following:

- Number of people visiting the library, if you have a way to track this; if not, electronic visitor trackers are available from library supply companies
- Number of collaborations with teachers, types of collaboration, and specific lessons planned, created, or taught
- Special events hosted by the library, such as literacy nights or student art exhibitions
- Programming, such as author visits, book club meetings, poetry slams, or contests
- Monthly resource acquisitions (types, amounts, costs)
- The monthly library calendar

Pamphlets

For events at which parents will be present, you may want to create a simple pamphlet about the library. This pamphlet lets parents learn a little about the library and read about the services it provides, but it also shows that you believe it is important to keep them informed about what you are doing for the school and their kids. Sections you might include are the following:

- Your contact information
- Procedures for book borrowing, computer use, etc.
- Upcoming events

Figure 4-2. Monthly Report

Library Report: January '09

visitors						
	morning		during school		Daily TOTAL	
Date:	North	South	North	South	North	South
January	4234	1645	8936	5738	13170	7383

Circulation Total for the month: 1110

Circulation Total year-to-date: 5141

LIBRARY EVENTS

Date:	Event:	N/S
1/18	Book club discussion meeting	N
1/22	Author Visit: Barry Lyga (all HS in attendance)	N

Hosted events (non-library):

Date:	Event:	N/S
1/3	English Dept Meeting	N
1/9	Student Council	N
1/9	Mentor meeting (ongoing)	S
1/9	SS Dept. meeting	N
1/10	Conflict Resolution	N
1/19	CKH follow-up	N
1/23	TAKS field test	N/S
1/24	Conflict Resolution	N
1/30	Teacher In-service (all day)	S
1/31	Principal's Round Table	N

Instructional Support

Date:	Teacher/Class assisted:	Action:
1/8	Techmanski	Designed lesson on Macbeth/Shakespeare, located resources, and created class project page.
1/15	Serrano	Designed lesson on Elizabethan concept of love and sonnets, located resources, and created class project page.
1/16	Singer	Designed lesson on nutrition, located resources, and created class project page.
1/22	Jones	Designed lesson for genetic defects and diseases, located resources, and created class project page.
1/24	Social Studies team	Met with the team to plan the upcoming research project
1/29 – 2/1	English II	Taught lesson on career project and database use; co-teach during research time

- Book lists, such as award winners, summer reading list, etc.
- Passwords for databases
- Links to recommended Web sites
- Information for parent volunteers

Phone and In-person Communication

With all of the new technologies that are available, don't forget that sometimes you simply will need to communicate with members of the school community in person. While teachers and students may not be immediately available for a phone call or discussion, you will need to recognize when it's appropriate to contact administrators, teachers, and colleagues via phone or to set up a meeting.

Locating and Learning about Important Documents

Certain documents will be important to you as the school's librarian. Some are philosophical, some are policy statements, and some are practical guidelines, but all of them will influence the way you do your job each day. In this chapter you will find brief explanations of some of the documents and policies with which you will need to become familiar; you will need to locate these documents in your school or on the Internet, as appropriate, or you will need to develop and write policies and documents if they do not already exist for your library.

Library Bill of Rights

This document by the American Library Association (ala.org) serves as a reminder that a librarian's task is to provide people with information and protect their rights to access it. The *Interpretation of the Library Bill of Rights* goes into further detail about censorship and the freedom to read (see Part VI, Selected Policy Documents).

Selection Policy

The selection policy is probably located in your district's policies, and your district library coordinator can get you a copy or show you how to access it online. Read through it now as it guides how you are to select materials for your library. A small district or private school may not have a policy in place. If not, you need to meet with some of your stakeholders and put one together. The selection policy ensures uniform standards when selecting books and other materials and can be used to defend the purchase of materials that are challenged. The policy should include what types of materials will be acquired, who will be responsible for selecting them, and how the materials are chosen (based on professional reviews, for example—these review sources should be listed in the policy). If your school or district does not have a selection policy in place, your first job is to create one. You will

IN THIS CHAPTER:
- ✔ Library Bill of Rights
- ✔ Selection Policy
- ✔ Reconsideration Policy for Challenged Material
- ✔ Electronic Communication and Data Management Policy
- ✔ Copyright Information
- ✔ Library Policy and Procedure Manual

WEB SITES RELATED TO SELECTION POLICY

Arizona State Library, Archives and Public Records. *Collection Development Training for Arizona Public Libraries. 2008.* http://www.lib.az.us/cdt

Baltimore County Public Schools. *Selection Criteria for School Library Media Center Collections.* http://www.bcps.org/offices/lis/office/admin/selection.html

California Department of Education. *District Selection Policies on Recommended Literature: K-12.* http://www.cde.ca.gov/ci/rl/ll/litrlppolicies.asp

Christa McAuliffe School Library. 2004. *Policy for Selection and Review of Library Materials.* http://www.cupertino.k12.ca.us/McAuliffe.www/Library/libmaterialselectionpolicy.pdf

Hopkinton High School and Hopkinton Middle School Library, Contoocook, New Hampshire (2005). *Selection Policy and Guidelines: Selection of Instructional Materials.* http://www.hopkinton schools.org/hhs/library/selpol.html

Iola-Scandinavia Middle/High School Library, Iola, Wisconsin. *District Selection Policy: Guidelines for the Selection of Library Media Center Materials.* http://www.iola.k12.wi.us/hs/districtselection.cfm

Konawaena High School, Kealakekua, Hawaii. *Materials Selection Policy.* http://www.k12.hi.us/~konawahs/materials_selection_policy.htm

Montana State Library. *Collection Development Policy Guidelines for School Library Media Programs.* http://msl.state.mt.us/slr/cmpolsch.html

Pitman High School Library Media Center, Turlock, California. *Library Selection Policy.* http://phs.turlock.k12.ca.us/pages/library/Library%20Selection%20Policy.htm

Resources for School Librarians. *Collection Development.* http://www.sldirectory.com/libsf/resf/coldev2.html

School District of Philadelphia Library Programs and Services. 2002. *Selection Policy for School Library Materials.* http://libraries.phila.k12.pa.us/misc/selection-policy.html

Weiner High School Library, Weiner, Arkansas. *Selection Policy for Library Materials.* http://cardinal.k12.ar.us/lib.site/Selection%20policy.htm

---

find many samples online by searching "school library policies and procedures" or "school library management."

Reconsideration Policy for Challenged Material

A reconsideration policy or procedure is crucial for protecting your school community's intellectual freedom. Book challenges most often occur because well-meaning parents react to books they feel are not appropriate for children to read; book removal or banning, however, is not the answer. The best way to deal with a challenge calmly and professionally is to have a policy and procedure in place. The reconsideration policy should state that books will not be immediately removed at the moment of challenge, that parents have the right to determine what is appropriate for their child only, and that there are steps in place for those individuals wishing to have a book's inclusion in the collection reconsidered. Those steps should be outlined, from initial challenge meeting to formal paperwork submission to committee review. Challenge forms and committee reporting forms should be included in the policy, and the policy should indicate who will be included in a review committee and should include an administrator, a librarian, a teacher, a representative from the community, and possibly a library administrator from another school district. The policy should also state how the committee will make its decision, and then make that decision known. Although you won't want to hand the policy or any forms to a parent the moment they bring a book to your attention, you will want to have those documents handy for reference in case a challenge should occur. A sample reconsideration form is shown in Figure 5-1, and you will find additional samples online at the American Library Association Office of Intellectual Freedom (www.ala.org/ala/aboutala/offices/oif/).

Electronic Communication and Data Management Policy

Also called an "acceptable use policy," this is a school or district document (not library specific) that outlines acceptable use of the school or district's resources and equipment. It includes specifications on e-mail usage, Internet access, copyright, and more. You need to keep a copy of this document because several of the items apply to you, such as photocopying of print materials and acceptable Internet use. An example of acceptable use policies for electronic resources is located in Selected Policy Documents, along with some suggested links to other well-crafted AUPs; you will find additional samples online by searching "acceptable use policy in schools."

Copyright Information

Copyright is going to be your area of expertise—whether you want it to be or not (see Figure 5-2). The librarian is usually the "copyright guru" in the

Figure 5-1. Request for Reconsideration of Instructional Materials

Name _____ Date _____

Address _____

City _____ State _____ Zip _____

Phone _____

Do you represent yourself? _____ an organization? _____ (If an organization, please identify:

_____)

Resource on which you are commenting:

_____ Book	_____ Magazine	_____ Audio recording
_____ Textbook	_____ Library program	_____ Newspaper
_____ Video/DVD	_____ Electronic information/network (please specify)	
_____ Display	_____ Other _____	

Title: _____

Author/Producer: _____

1. Have you reviewed the materials in their entirety? If not, please do so before completing and submitting this form.

2. To what in the material do you object? (Please be specific: cite pages, etc.)

   _____

3. What do you believe might be the result of using this material?

   _____

4. For what age group would you recommend this material?

   _____

5. In its place, what material of equal quality would you recommend that could be used to teach similar subject matter?

   _____

6. What do you believe should be done with the material in question?

   _____ Remove it from the curriculum.

   _____ Do not allow my child to use this material.

   _____ Use it as resource material or a choice selection.

Complainant signature _____ Date _____

building. Luckily, you've probably already received training on copyright law and fair use. Information is available with specifications on copyright, like the U.S. Copyright Office's Web site at http://www.copyright.gov/. A recommended book on the topic is *Smart Copyright Compliance for Schools: A How-To-Do-It Manual* (Butler, 2009). It would also benefit you and the staff if you would create a simple informational flyer or pamphlet with brief, useful, "must know" information about copyright in schools. Be sure to

Figure 5-2. Copyright Pamphlet

Copyright in Schools

…what you need to know about the ethics and the law

"Democracy doesn't mean we get to pick and choose the laws we obey"

See the librarian for answers to specific questions or for more information

Copyright Specifics by Format

Print

-single copies-
- a chapter from a book
- an article
- a short story, essay, or poem
  (entire poem of 250 words or 10 % or less of a longer work)
- a chart, graph, diagram, or drawing
- must be exact copies, not derivatives

-multiple copies-
- no more than one copy per student
- must contain a copyright notice
- not from consumables (workbooks)
- not to substitute for purchase
- not to be used year after year

* creations of new anthologies are not permitted, like taking favorite poems and compiling them into a booklet.

Videos

- must be a legal copy (bought or rented)
- may not be copied!
- performance must be in classroom, not in an auditorium, cafeteria, bus, etc.
- performance must be directed by a teacher or student, not just broadcasted
- performance must be used in face-to-face instruction, not a reward or free time
- off-air recordings of broadcasts may be used but must be erased 45 days after original broadcast

Graphics

Must not be used for profit (can't be placed on items for sale, like shirts, bumper stickers, candy-grams, etc.), and must be exact copies, not derivatives…which means no enlarging and then tracing/sketching and no altering (like copying a character and adding a shirt with the school mascot).

Public Performance

Music, drama, dance, motion pictures, and other works may not be performed publicly without written permission unless the rules for fair use are followed (see Videos). Student performances may not be recorded and then sold or published online.

Software

- may not be copied
- may only be saved on one computer unless a site license is obtained
- may not be "shared" or networked unless a site license is obtained

FINAL NOTES…

The library and workroom staff will not knowingly violate copyright law and will, for everyone's protection, educate in order to prevent the school from committing violations and risking lawsuits. More information is available in the book Copyright for Schools by Carol Simpson (available in the library).

What is Copyright?

Copyright is the protection of intellectual property (any form of expression placed in durable form - written on paper, recorded, painted, crafted, coded into a computer, etc.). A work does not have to have a notice of copyright or a copyright symbol (©) to be protected by law. Assume all works created after 1978 are protected by copyright.

Copyright Info Online:

http://www.copyright.gov/

Rights of the Copyright Holder

The creator of the work holds the rights to (which means you may not do these without permission):

- reproduction
- adaptation (changing from one format to another, like turning a poem or story into a play or song)
- distribution of copies
- public performance
- public display
- digital transmission (like placing on a Web page or file-transferring)

Public Domain

Seventy years after the death of its creator, a work is considered "public domain" and is no longer protected by copyright laws.

Educational Protection a.k.a. "Fair Use"

Copyright law was amended to give schools special exceptions to the strict laws. HOWEVER, fair use is not intended to allow infringement of the law. Schools can and do still get into trouble for copyright violation. Certain guidelines must be met to qualify for fair use protection:

∞ must be for nonprofit purpose
∞ must have no effect on the potential market for / value of the work
∞ copying/production occurs at the instance and inspiration of the individual teacher, not from a supervisor (and not in anticipation of need – no "just in case")
∞ the inspiration & decision to use the work **and** the moment for its use are so close in time that obtaining permission is unreasonable/impossible

Breaking the Law

Damages awarded to the creators of a work can run in the hundreds of thousands of dollars. Lawsuits don't only affect the violator but can go up the chain of command to librarians, principals, curriculum coordinators, superintendents, and school board members. Copyright lawsuits are becoming more frequent.

Works Protected by Copyright

∞ Literary Works (books, poems, short stories, plays, magazine and newspaper articles, etc.)

∞ Audio Visuals (photographs, paintings, emblems/logos, graphics, videos, films, DVDs, performances, live speeches, broadcasts, audio recordings, etc.)

∞ Electronic Resources (software, Web pages, Internet, e-mail, etc.)

Students Own Copyrights!

Your students own copyrights on their own works. You may not publish, reproduce, or display (outside of classroom use) a student's work without obtaining permission from the student or his/her parents (if a minor). You may not keep student work for future use or display without written permission since the student won't be involved in the instructional use of the work.

Top-Down Directives

A directive from a supervisor for use of copyrighted materials OR the dispersion of copyrighted materials by a supervisor to staff members whether for professional review or instructional use is not protected by fair use and is considered illegal.

Figure 5-3. Copyright Statement for Posting Near Photocopiers or in a Media Center

Copyright

©

The copyright law of the United States (Title 17 U.S. Code) governs the making of photocopies or other reproductions of copyrighted material.

This institution reserves the right to refuse to accept a copying order if, in its judgment, fulfillment of the order would involve violation of copyright law.

post a statement near each photocopier in your library that states the copyright law (see Figure 5-3) just in case you are asked to reproduce something that would be in violation of the copyright law.

Library Policy and Procedure Manual

The previous list presents selected documents, but they serve as examples of what must be documented. All of the important documents that you have located and gathered, and those that you have written yourself (or will write) that are related to library policies and procedures need to be collected and placed into a library policy and procedure manual (see Figure 5-4); if a manual already exists, make sure that everything is up to date. This manual can be in print format, but should also be available electronically so that your administration and teachers can have access to it (school districts have intranets that will allow you to make these documents available to authorized personnel). Don't forget to have administration and the school board approve any new or updated policies.

Written policies and procedures will inform your school community of everything from the length of time a book can be checked out and library hours to procedures for reserving audiovisual equipment and how to place an order for a book. Where appropriate (for example, the use of computers in the library), school policy might take precedence, and that policy needs to be part of your library policy and procedure manual. To the school policy on computer use, which will deal with inappropriate use of or damage to computers, you might add specific library policies, such as the length of time a computer in the library can be used by one student if another student is waiting. A well-written policy will allow you to enforce rules equitably and will help you and your library staff maintain order and effectively handle the library's business.

Reference

Butler, R. 2009. *Smart Copyright Compliance for Schools: A How-To-Do-It Manual.* New York: Neal-Schuman.

Figure 5-4. Content Outline for a Library Policy and Procedure Manual

Introduction
—Purpose of Library Policy and Procedure Manual
—Mission Statement of the School Library Media Center

School and Community Analysis

Overview of School Library Media Collection
—Print Materials
—Audiovisual Materials
—Electronic/Digital Media/Online Resources

Material Selection Policy
—Responsibility for Selection
— Teachers, Students, Parents Recommendations for Library Media Center Materials

Selection Criteria for Library Media Center Materials
—Criteria for Print Materials and Non-print Materials
—Selection Tools and Reviewing Resources

Acquisitions
—Format Considerations
—Automating Acquisitions
—Selecting and Evaluating Vendors
—Participation in Cooperative Acquisitions

Cataloging and Classification
—Placement of Materials

Gifts and Donations

Collection Maintenance and Preservation

Weeding Library Media Collection
—Criteria for Weeding

Budgeting

Copyright

Acceptable Internet Use

Inventory

Scheduling

Circulation
—Teacher Use
—Student Use
—Other Faculty and staff

Reconsideration of Library Media Center Materials
—Procedures for Handling Challenged Materials

Confidentiality
—Procedures for Handling Censorship and/or Government-sponsored Investigations

Evaluation, Periodic Review and Policy Revision

Forms
—Faculty Recommendations for Library Media Center Materials
—Student and Parent Recommendations for Library Media Center
—Materials
—Request for Reconsideration of Materials

Appendices
—Code of Ethics of the American Library Association
—Library Bill of Rights
—Freedom to Read Statement
—Freedom to View Statement

Library Media Specialist as Library Administrator

This is the aspect of your job with which most people are familiar (even though you will do much more). If you were at a social gathering and people were making small talk about family and careers, what image would pop into their heads when you said you were a librarian? It would be the image of library administrator—the person who runs the place and takes care of the books. If you don't already realize it, you will read in subsequent chapters how your job entails so much more than administrating the library. This part, however, will cover some of the tasks you will perform and decisions you will make in the management of the library. The school's library is like a place of business, and you are the boss. As the boss, you are responsible for supervising the staff, overseeing the budget, and making sure the shelves are stocked with quality books and other materials that your school community will use and appreciate. You basically make all of the decisions about how the library will run on a daily basis and then make sure it is run that way.

As you read the chapters in this part, keep in mind that a well-oiled machine will continue to run smoothly without constant tweaking. The more organized you are and the more structured and routine the basic library functions become, the easier these tasks will be, and the less time you will spend on them. It is natural to spend quite a bit of time on the administrative parts of your job at the beginning, especially when you are a new librarian. As time goes on, however, if you feel that you are spending a majority of your time in the "librarian as administrator" role, you may need to keep a log of tasks you perform during the day. Record the log for a few days and make sure you keep track of the amount of time you spend at each task. After a few days, divide your tasks each day into the three roles of a school librarian and calculate percentages; the administrative part of your job should take up about 15 to 20 percent of your day on average.

Staffing the Library

To misquote an old proverb, "It takes a village to run a library." Okay, maybe this is a bit of an exaggeration. However, if you are the only one working in your school library, it will be a struggle for you. In the best cases, you will be given support staff and volunteers to help you with the daily tasks of running the library. In times of financial difficulties, administration may be less supportive of the library; in those situations, you need to be prepared to work with less paid staff and to use staff creatively. This chapter will help you evaluate the types of staff you need and how to use them effectively.

Paraprofessionals

The person who can do the most to help you make everything run smoothly in your library is the library paraprofessional/assistant/aide (different titles are used in different schools). He or she should be taking care of most of the clerical work so that you can focus on administration and educational collaboration. The paraprofessional acts as your other pair of hands. Your assistant may have a college degree, some college hours, technical training, or clerical experience. Depending on the level of education, skills, and training, your assistant can take care of such tasks as running the circulation desk, book maintenance, shelving, paperwork, processing, computer support, point-of-need instruction, and record keeping. It is important that you have a good working relationship with this person as he or she can help alleviate a large portion of the workload in the library, freeing you to work with teachers and instruct students.

If you have the opportunity to interview the person who will be your assistant, be sure to explain your expectations. List the duties he or she will be performing on a daily basis as well as additional tasks that may come up during the year. Describe some situations that may occur in the library and ask how he or she would handle them or how he or she handled similar situations in the past. Figure 6-1 shows a job description for a library assistant.

Figure 6-1. Library Assistant Job Description Sample	

TITLE:	Library Aide
QUALIFICATIONS:	High school graduate or equivalent (GED) Qualifies for appropriate state paraprofessional certification Keyboarding ability
REPORTS TO:	Principal and librarian assigned
JOB GOAL:	To assist teachers and students in the effective use of the media center as a learning resource

RESPONSIBILITIES:

1. Helps teachers and students locate both print and non-print materials.
2. Maintains day-to-day circulation of materials using library management software.
3. Organizes and shelves materials.
4. Inputs student data into automated library circulation system and Accelerated Reader.
5. Understands and operates the management component of the library circulation software.
6. Operates the library online public access catalog (OPAC) used in student searches.
7. Enters materials acquisitions data.
8. Does troubleshooting maintenance of campus hardware: computers, printers, VCRs, laser players, televisions, overhead projectors, etc.
9. Demonstrates/operates appropriate audiovisual hardware when requested by students or staff: CD-ROM, computer, laser player, VCR, satellite, network navigation, video delivery, etc.
10. Prints overdue lists, barcodes, and bibliographies.
11. Processes books for student use.
12. Reads to students.
13. Maintains proper storage of media: books, periodicals, CD-ROM, DVDs, video cassettes, CDs, audiocassettes, and software.
14. Promotes an inviting learning environment; monitors student behavior in the library.
15. Organizes Region IV deliveries and online ordering of desired teaching materials.
16. Manages the library in the absence of the librarian.
17. Performs other responsibilities as the principal may assign.

You and your assistant should have positive interaction and work well together. You are this person's supervisor, but it is also important that the assistant feel valued. Recognize his or her hard work and willingness to go the extra mile. If your assistant is interested in learning some new skills and would like to take on some different tasks, embrace that. The more knowledgeable and versatile your assistant, the better and stronger team the two of you will be.

Adult Volunteers

With limited money, school districts may not be able to afford to provide you with full-time or even part-time help. This is where volunteer workers can come in handy. If you are fortunate enough to have library volunteers, utilize their help; if you don't have volunteers, seek out ways to locate them and to develop a network of helpers.

Some school libraries have several volunteers who alternate days in which they come in to assist the librarian; many schools, however, are experiencing a steady decline in parent and community involvement. Schools that do have volunteers often schedule them to work as teachers' aides, so the library might not be lucky enough to be assigned any volunteers. Make sure that your school administration knows that you want to have volunteer help and work with your school to help recruit volunteers who will be interested in being assigned to the library. Consider asking for volunteers in your newsletter or on your Web page.

Your volunteers will most likely be parents or community/business members who have undergone screening and background checks with the school or district. They will probably be able to work only certain days and hours. The best thing about volunteers is that they are willing and happy to help you in any way possible, and they are in your library because they want to be there. Make them feel appreciated and that you value their time and work. Do not make them feel as though they are a burden because they will take the hint and leave.

Start out by finding what the volunteer is willing and able to do. Some may have special skills or interests that can be of great help to you, such as the following:

- Computer skills—they can create flyers, posters, newsletters, help with the Web page, etc.
- Talented speaker—they can take over some of your story times.
- Artistic—they can be in charge of decorating or displays.
- Avid reader—they can do booktalks or recommended book lists.
- Party planner—they can help coordinate events and programs.

Let volunteers take on only what they are comfortable with and willing to do. If they seem bored by routine tasks you give them, such as book shelving, offer them projects, such as those listed previously. Drop them a thank-you card or host a luncheon in their honor. These volunteers value the library enough to give their time to help you, so show them you value that commitment.

Student Helpers

In lower elementary grades, you might select a student in each class to help during visits with circulation or a returned-book collection. In intermediate, middle, and high school libraries, however, you may have student helpers. Sometimes they choose to work in the library, and sometimes they do not. These students may be volunteers who assist you during nonclass times (like before and after school) or could be assigned to your library during certain periods of the school day. During their time with you, they should have the opportunity to learn some new skills and assist you in whatever ways they can.

Although it may seem at first as though you have taken on babysitting duty, in actuality this could be a great situation for you. If they are volunteers, they chose to be in the library because they are avid readers or are interested in the workings of the library. If they are assigned to you, they will strive to do well because they probably receive some sort of grade by you for performing their duties and being cooperative. Either way, you have a young person who is—or can become—a library supporter and can take on some of the work in the library that usually takes you away from your other many tasks.

The tasks you can assign a student helper depend on grade level and ability. They can run errands and deliver materials and paperwork within the building, shelve books, work the circulation desk, set up displays, assist with book repair and processing, and help other students locate materials or use computers and equipment within the library. Interview students and find out about their skills and interests. Be sure to train them on general library rules and procedures as well as procedures for completing tasks they will be assigned. Treat them as young adults in a real job; give them a contract or agreement to sign at the beginning of their "employment" that states duties and responsibilities (see Figure 6-2). Be sure to give student helpers positive feedback and constructive criticism and reassess their assignments periodically, adding or reducing responsibilities as needed.

Figure 6-2. Student Helper Agreement

Library Student Aide Contract and Information Sheet

Welcome! We are excited to have you as a library student aide this semester. This can be a fun experience for you. You will have the chance to learn the collection, help maintain a good working library, and work with adults in the building in a new capacity.

The most important thing in making this a good experience for you is attitude. Coming in each day with a positive and cooperative attitude, ready to work, and bringing new ideas to share with the librarians will make this a class you will enjoy. Remember, *this is a class*. Your duties are your assignments, the librarians are your teachers, and your grade is based on your performance just as in an academic class.

Daily Duties:
1. Empty the book return box.
2. Stamp one set of due-date cards.
3. Place returned books in order on book rack.
4. Shelve books in your assigned area: _____.
5. While shelving, straighten books and tidy your shelves.
6. Check library mailbox.
7. Straighten magazine/reading area.

Other duties could include:
1. Staff the circulation desk.
2. Help decorate library and set up displays.
3. Placing notices, flyers, etc., in teacher boxes.
4. Water library plants.
5. Assist other staff members.
- If you've completed duties and have extra time, you may do homework or read magazines or books.

Library student aide violations:
- Tardiness
- Leaving the library without permission
- Entering the back office without permission
- Using the library phones
- Leaving at the end of the period with your student aide badge

Violation of items on this contract or any other rules or procedures set by the librarians will result in disciplinary procedures, which could include the following:
- Lowering grade for this class
- Restrictions
- Referral to office
- Removal from student aide position

Student name: _____

Signature: _____

Working with Your Budget

You are now responsible for a sum of money that is not really yours. The sum could be tens of thousands of dollars, allowing you to purchase all sorts of materials and implement rich programming, or it could be a few hundred dollars, which barely allows you to purchase a few books and forces you to be creative in what you buy and do for your school and how you pay for it. Either way, you are expected to correctly and efficiently spend the money you are budgeted and account for every penny of it.

Budget Funds versus Activity Funds

First, it is important to understand the difference between the types of money included in your budget. This is especially important in public schools and with federal funds. Budget funds are allotted to your school and in turn to your library by a governing entity, such as the school district, which gets it from the state or city. Budget funds also have certain restrictions:

- These funds are given each academic year and must be spent during that academic year or they are lost.

- The money is tightly controlled in that certain funds can be spent only on certain types of items (for example, book money cannot be used to purchase computers).

- Purchases can be made only with approved or committed vendors.

- Expenditures must be approved and go through a purchase-order process.

Budget funds are often categorized as line item or lump sum budgets; check to see which type of budget your school district uses as you will need to set up your records according to their procedure. Line-item budgets allocate a certain amount of money for broad categories of purchases such as books, periodicals, and supplies; money will be allotted for each broad category. With a lump-sum budget, your library will be given a single allocation for all purchases. Since this allows you to decide how much money to spend on books, periodicals, supplies, etc., it is preferred over a line-item budget. However, you probably will need to do a bit more planning to be sure you don't spend all of your money on books, for example, and neglect audiovisuals.

Activity funds are those funds you amass through library income, such as fines and book fairs. These funds remain in an account until used. They have fewer restrictions and can be used more flexibly (for example, you can go to local discount stores and purchase items at lower costs and then be reimbursed from your activity fund account). Fund-raisers to increase your activity fund are discussed later in this chapter.

Keeping Good Records

For both budget and activity accounts, it is important that you maintain accurate and complete records. This will help you determine how much funding you have available at any given time and will help you discover accounting errors. These records must also be available in case of an audit. Keeping good financial records is easy if you start with a procedure in place and follow it. Be sure to explain the procedure to your assistant if he or she will be working with any part of the budget or purchasing.

Your records should be maintained via an Excel (or equivalent) spreadsheet; however, you will still want to maintain print records. For record-keeping, you will need a large three-ring binder. Label it "Finances" and include the school year (e.g., "2009–2010"). Add dividers for each account you have. An easy way to label dividers is with budgetary category or budget code. Make sure you include dividers for any activity account you may have. On the inside front cover or pocket attach a listing of all accounts along with the starting amount for the year in each account.

Next, you will need to create an electronic spreadsheet for each account that you will use. If you don't already know how to create an electronic spreadsheet, ask your technology specialist or computer teacher to show you how to use the software to set up your spreadsheet; having an electronic sheet will make accounting simple and organized. Be sure to include the categories (like "Furniture" and "Books"), the account numbers or budget codes, and the starting amounts. Leave some rows for transactions in each category, and then create "Total" cells, which calculate the balances for each category. See Figure 7-1 for an example.

You are now set up for the year. Each time you make a transaction, whether a purchase or deposit, follow these steps:

- Open your electronic spreadsheet and enter the transaction description, date, and amount (positive for deposits, negative for purchases); pay attention to the "Total" for that category or account and make sure it changes accordingly—otherwise you have a formula error.

- Gather any order forms and copies of purchase orders, punch holes in them, and file them in the finance binder behind the appropriate divider. If the transaction is a deposit, file the deposit slip (if it's a deposit, you are done at this point).

Figure 7-1. Budget Spreadsheet Sample

Books		
555-01-6328-02-002-9-12-00X		
opening balance (August 2008)		$ 8,000.00
ABC Bookstore	3-Jan	-458.25
TOTAL:		$ 7,541.75
Magazines / Books		
555-01-6329-02-002-9-12-00X		
opening balance (August 2008)		$ 2,000.00
TOTAL:		$ 2,000.00
Warehouse		
555-01-6397-02-002-9-12-00X		
opening balance (August 2008)		$ 1,400.00
printer paper and toner cartridges	27-Apr	-232.60
TOTAL:		$ 1,167.40
General		
555-01-6399-02-002-9-12-00X		
opening balance (August 2007)		$ 3,500.00
XYZ Furnishings Inc.	17-Mar	-1,250.82
TOTAL:		$ 2,249.18
Technology/Software		
555-01-6396-02-002-9-12-00X		
opening balance (August 2007)		$ 1,500.00
TOTAL:		$ 1,500.00

- When the order is received and you have verified the items, match the purchase amount on the paperwork to the amount you entered in your electronic spreadsheet.

- Gather any receipts, invoices, or packing slips, punch holes in them, and place them in the finance binder behind the appropriate divider.

- If it is the procedure, send paperwork and/or receiving verification to the appropriate school district purchasing or finance personnel.

- *At the end of the year* print out your electronic spreadsheet and place it in the binder. Your accounting is neat, organized, and done.

Fund-raising

Aside from collecting fines from overdue materials (which is discussed briefly in the next chapter), you can generate additional funding for your library in some other ways. These funds go into an activity account and can be used to purchase books, furnishings, equipment, supplies, etc. In schools with limited budgets, fund-raising may be necessary to pay for the cost of normal operations and programming. As always, keep accurate financial records. Also, it is a good idea to publicize information about how funds will be spent—people are more likely to donate if they know the money will be spent on buying better books for students, for example. Some suggested fund-raisers are the following:

- Book fairs: A book fair company will send you cases of books that you can sell to students, teachers, parents, etc., and will give you a percentage of sales in money or books. Book fairs can be fun and will help you to get books into your students' hands and homes, but they are also a lot of work. Contact book fair companies and begin gathering information. Enlist some volunteers to help with setup, sales, monitoring, and teardown. Promote the event (companies will send you promotional materials) and try to schedule it during a time when parents will be in the building, like an open house or parents' night.

- "Donated by" books: A great way to acquire more books for your library is to allow students, teachers, and parents to purchase materials in honor of someone special to them (or in honor of themselves). You can simply have preset amounts—$5, $10, $25, $50—and purchase titles later or you can generate a list of books needed/wanted and allow donators to choose the title(s) they wish to donate. Collect funds before ordering the books, then create book plates when the shipment arrives. After processing all books and affixing donation plates, hold a celebration and invite everyone (especially donators) to come and see all of the new books. Promote this event in-house and with mailers or flyers; send them to parents and post them in the community.

- Old book sale: Old books donated by staff, students, and parents or purchased with activity funds can be displayed on carts and sold at a set cost (50¢ or $1 per book). Request donations for the old book sale and have a place to box them when they arrive. At the sale, arrange the books by general subject. Publicize the sale with flyers and signs. Have a plan for unsold books, like donation to a charity or recycling. Note: Books from your library that are purchased with budget funds cannot be sold as a fund-raiser. Find out the proper procedure for disposal of old materials purchased with budget funds (see Chapter 9 for more details).

- "Reading Is Fundamental" (RIF): This is a federally sponsored program that partners with organizations and schools to provide free books to at-risk children who may not otherwise have books at home. Your school must provide matching funds (at least 25 percent). You would order titles or sets that would arrive for distribution to your students. Setup should be similar to a book fair where students can browse and choose a book; RIF has three distribution events per year. Although this program does not provide more materials for your library, it is a great way to provide reading materials to your students and to get them excited about reading.

Circulating Books and Other Materials

Books—that's what most people think of when they think of a library. The availability of books for borrowing and returning is the main reason a library was built for your school. Your predecessors and you put a lot of time and effort into selecting materials to include in the collection that students and staff would find useful and enjoyable (see Chapter 10 for more information about book selection). Having good materials on the shelves is important for attracting library users; now you must make some decisions about how those materials are going to flow out of and back into your library.

Manual and Automated Procedures

If you work in a small school library or are not part of a district, you may still be using a manual or paper system for checkout. Your books would have a circulation card in the pocket which would allow for handwritten entry of a student's name and room number or a teacher's name. The student would turn in that card for record-keeping purposes and take a prestamped date due card or slip and place it in the pocket as a reminder. If you have an assistant or volunteer, this person may be the one who takes the cards and gives students the date due slips. Those cards would then be organized and filed so that you can keep track of materials that are checked out and the return date.

Most schools will have an automated system that not only maintains the records of all materials (in place of a shelf list or card catalog) but also takes care of the circulation process. The student or your assistant scans the identifying barcode and the barcode on the books being checked out. A date due slip or receipt is given to the student, or a date due sticker can be affixed on the front or back cover. The automated system keeps track of items checked out and returned, borrower accounts, and due dates on all materials. Although expensive and at-risk for occasional technical glitches, automated systems drastically reduce human error and the time spent on circulation, inventory, borrower records, and catalog maintenance. One benefit of automated systems is the availability of borrower records during circulation, which makes it easier to identify students or others who have overdue books or those who may owe book fines or have restrictions on checkout (see Figure 8-1). If you are considering installing or changing automated systems for your library, make a list of features desired and then do some research; system vendors will often allow you trial access to the software, a visit from a salesperson to demonstrate features, and references you can contact who are currently using the system.

Length of Time for Circulation

Every librarian needs to make decisions about the length of time that a book or other material will circulate. The school district may have circulation policies already in place, but this does not mean you can't make changes or suggestions for different circulation time periods. Work with school

Figure 8-1. Circulation Screen in Automated System

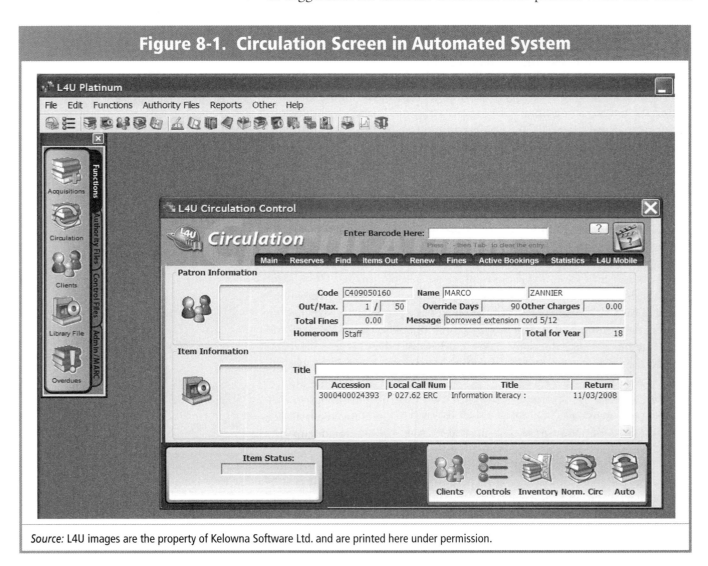

Source: L4U images are the property of Kelowna Software Ltd. and are printed here under permission.

administration and teachers to implement the circulation time that best serves your school community.

Age level and other demographics of the population served by the school district will affect the length of time that a book should circulate. Younger students (kindergarten, for example) can finish reading a book in a day, so a week would probably be more than enough time for a checkout. Older students (middle and high school) who check out novels would probably need two weeks or more. Some high schools use even longer checkout periods in order to reduce issues of overdues and fines. After you determine the standard checkout period for your library, consider these special circumstances:

- Faculty: They will require longer periods of time for checkout because they are probably using materials for planning, research, instruction, or read-aloud. Your library might give faculty members indefinite checkout periods, but you might consider a more finite period, such as three months or a school marking period, just so that you will eventually notice an overdue and be able to check with faculty members to see if they still require the materials. With longer checkouts, some faculty members will forget they have materials out until you notice it, and you don't want them to be scrambling to search for those materials on the last day of school.

- Periodicals: Your library might keep magazines and newspapers scattered in a lounge-type area for use in the library; if so, decide if, when, and how those materials will be circulated. Keep in mind that if you check out current materials for two-week periods, they will no longer be of any use by the time they are returned since a new magazine issue will be arriving. You might consider short-term circulation (a day, two days, or a week) on new magazines. Old magazines, if not archived, can be given away or discarded, depending on school district policy. Newspapers are of little use the next day unless there is a particular international, national, or local news event that is of interest in your school; if this is the case, you might just save that particular article in a vertical file for checkout, or, alternatively, scan the article and save it as an electronic file rather than creating a vertical file, if space is a problem. Remember, also, that most newspapers are now available online, with older issues often accessible for free.

- Equipment: Expensive pieces of technology will probably be available only to faculty for circulation. Some devices (like digital cameras) should have shorter checkout periods depending on the number of items available to your faculty. Larger items that will be used on a long-term basis (like overhead projectors or document cameras) should have longer checkout periods. In a manual system, create cards for each item as you would for books; use those to keep track of which faculty member has the item and when it was checked out. You might also keep a chart on which faculty members write the periods during which they will have the equipment so that others who need it can schedule lessons accordingly. In an automated system, equipment can be barcoded and circulated the

AUTOMATION SOURCES

Capterra, Inc.
http://www.capterra.com/library-automation-software

COMPanion Corporation
http://www.goalexandria.com/

Information Today Inc.
http://www.infotoday.com/MMSchools/jul04/fiehn.shtml

Surpass Software
http://www.surpasssoftware.com/

SirsiDynix
http://www.sirsidynix.com/

Follett Software Company
http://www.fsc.follett.com/

same way as books. The computer makes it easy to track who has the item, when it is due, and when it will be available.

- Vertical file: If you keep items, such as pamphlets, newspaper clippings, etc., in a vertical file, then you will need a way to circulate them. Whether they are for in-library use only or you will allow the items to be taken for use outside of the library, a simple card system will help you keep track of who is using it and when. Decide how long the item can be taken from the premises—one day is probably long enough. In an automated system, the items can be placed in envelopes, folders, or clear protectors with barcodes that can be scanned as borrowers check them out. You can eliminate the need for a vertical file by scanning ephemeral material such as pamphlets and newspaper clippings and creating electronic files of these materials. Rather than circulating the items, users can access them from the library's Web page, for example.

- Audiovisuals: Items like DVDs and software might be available to just faculty or to all library users. If students are allowed to check them out, a shorter period of time is recommended in order to reduce the risk of loss or damage. Teachers, on the other hand, may need them for several weeks for use in their classrooms. Whether you use a manual or automated system, the same procedures can be used with AV as with books (due date cards or barcodes).

- Renewals: You must also decide if items can be renewed and for what time period. Your students might benefit from being able to renew materials they already have checked out, especially if they are checking out research books for a project or lengthy novels. If you will allow renewal, decide how many times a student can renew an item and what will happen if a reservation or "hold" is placed on an item. For example, your policy might be that if another borrower requests the item then the individual who currently has the item checked out cannot renew it (see section on reserves later in this chapter).

Overdues and Fines

Decide on your overdue policy and make it known to students and parents from the beginning. Overdue policies are often more lenient at the elementary and intermediate grades but stricter at middle and high school levels where students should be more responsible about borrowing materials. If you are using a manual system, your overdue notices will take much more time and you may need to do them less frequently. Automated systems will automatically produce overdue reports, so you can send out notifications weekly (more often than that may not be time or cost-efficient). After sending several notices to the same borrower, you might consider something more formal that you have created and possibly signed which can be sent to the student or mailed home (see Figure 8-2 for a sample letter). It is a good public relations move not to send overdue notices to faculty for items they have out; instead, send them a reminder if the item has been out for several months or a personal request if another faculty member needs the material. If you are posting overdues in the library or hallway, use a code system, such as student ID numbers, and be sure not to include personal information like names, social security numbers, etc.—after all, confidentiality of borrower information is supported by the American Library Association. Also, do not post the titles of materials that students have checked out and overdue. While this policy may seem a bit unnecessary, imagine a student has checked out a book about teen pregnancy or homosexuality. Posting titles that a student has not returned is a breach of confidentiality and weakens your position as information provider.

Another decision you must make is whether or not to charge fines. If you are in an elementary school and almost every student has overdue books and it takes months to get them back, fines may do more damage than good. If you are at a high school and have trouble with getting books returned because students are being lazy about dropping them into the return slot, fines might help reduce the problem. Most schools charge between a nickel and a quarter per day, and most have a cap on the amount that can be owed (for example, $5.00 is a good amount). The threat of fines keeps some students from ever checking out books, but it also teaches

Figure 8-2. Sample Overdue Notice

Student: _____ Homeroom: _____

Our records show that you have one or more books overdue. The title(s) and due date(s) are:

BOOK TITLE:	DUE DATE:

Our system indicates that we have sent _____ notifications. As of today's date, you owe a total of $ _____ in fines (fines increase 25¢ per day per book); fines can be cleared using "Ram Bucks." Your account has been blocked, so you will not be able to check out any more books until your record is clear. Please locate and return the book(s) listed above as soon as possible. Accounts with books overdue for two months or more result in a report card hold and a letter sent home to parents asking for their assistance in the matter.

If you have any questions about this letter, please speak to the library information specialist.

Marco Zannier
EHS Library Information Specialist

responsibility and is a source of income for the library. Think about the population you serve and the benefits and disadvantages of charging fines, then decide what will work best at your school.

In addition to fines, many school districts will not release report cards until all fines are paid and overdue materials returned. At the end of each marking period, the librarian will be asked for a list of students with outstanding books or fines owed. Check with your school district administration to see whether this policy is in effect.

Reserves (Placing an Item "on Hold")

Some materials, because of popularity or a common unit of study in your school, may become hot items for checkout. If students or faculty are looking for items that are currently checked out, consider allowing them to place a reserve on the item. If you use a manual system for circulation, you will need to decide on a way to indicate that a reserve has been requested (for example, by writing on the item's card, clipping to it the name of the person placing the reserve, or creating a colored card that will temporarily replace the item's true card until it is returned). An automated system makes reserving an item fast and simple. On entering the borrower's name and item desired, a "flag" is placed on the item's record. When the item is scanned in on return, a message notifies you that the item has been reserved and who has requested it. You can probably even print out the notification from that screen. Whether you use a manual or automated system, always notify the person who placed the reserve that the item has been returned and is ready for checkout. For faculty members, a quick e-mail or a notification in their box works well; for students, you might send a notification to their homeroom class.

Automated systems allow much greater flexibility in dealing with reserves than a manual system. For example, an automated system can issue a recall notice for an item that is currently checked out but has had a reserve placed on it; the item might then be called back early or the borrower notified that he or she can keep the item until the due date, but that a renewal will not be allowed. All of these notices can usually be generated automatically by an automated system.

Allow for Flexibility

A word of caution: It's important that your policies and procedures be available and known to everyone who uses your library. Posting circulation time periods, fines, reserve policy, and more makes it much easier to enforce your rules. However, you have the power to change the rules or to make exceptions. In cases where an error has been made or something was unclear to the borrower, leniency is in order—it's just good public relations.

Weeding and Doing Inventory

Although librarians know that weeding improves the collection, educators and taxpayers most likely will not understand why weeding is done and may consider it a waste of money. To a nonlibrarian, weeding looks like the wacky librarian is throwing away perfectly good books again. Weeding is a necessary process that prevents the library from becoming a stale and decaying wasteland of useless materials. As much as it pains librarians to throw books in the recycling bin, they do it because they know it is the right thing to do.

Why Should You Weed?

Imagine that you take your mail out of your mailbox every day and drop it into a large empty box in your kitchen. Each day you pile on more mail, whether it is a bill, a letter from your grandmother, or an advertisement from a furniture store. Now imagine you were going to be out of the country for a few weeks and you asked your trusted neighbor to pay your cell phone bill from the past month because the provider has threatened to disconnect you. He needs a particular piece of information—your cell phone bill from the past month—but he can't find it because he is digging through other old bills, junk mail, and personal correspondence. If he comes across a phone bill from three months ago, he would not have the current amount due, so he would have to call the company using the information from the old bill and hope they would give him the new information after he stays on hold for 45 minutes. After digging through all of your old mail, he would probably throw all of the junk back into the box and give up.

This is why librarians weed the materials in the library. If they didn't, the shelves would be so cluttered with outdated and useless materials that library users would have trouble finding what they needed, and they would give up.

What Should Be Weeded?

The most obvious items to weed are those that are aged, worn, torn, and damaged beyond repair. Keeping these items only makes the shelves look untidy, and items with water damage or high humidity exposure can promote the growth of mold, which will spread to other books in your library. Also weed materials that do not circulate and are not useful to your school community; even though these materials may be in great condition, they have no value if they are not part of the curriculum or are not of any interest to your students. If you have duplicates of items that are only occasionally checked out, weed all but one copy. If you have books in a set or series, like an encyclopedia or a fictional trilogy, that are missing several volumes or books, decide if you will replace the missing items in order to complete the set or weed the remaining volumes.

Currency and accuracy are important characteristics of good library materials. Items that are outdated should be weeded and replaced with newer resources. Weed items that contain incorrect information (like countries that no longer exist), outmoded references or photos, and information or representations that are offensive and inappropriate (like derogatory racial terms as references for a group or negative ethnic stereotypes). Use the following general guide as a starting point for determining when items in each Dewey Decimal category should be evaluated and removed.

- **000s:** 3–5 years. Encyclopedias, almanacs, and books about technology and computers should be weeded sooner.
- **100s:** 5–7 years. Watch for dated photos and weed trendy self-help or motivational books as they lose popularity.
- **200s:** 5–7 years. Add materials as needed to offer various viewpoints and beliefs, and weed uncirculated duplicates.
- **300s:** 3–5 years. Folklore needs little weeding; pay closer attention to books on politics, economics, social issues, and careers.
- **400s:** 7–10 years. Little weeding is needed in a language section except for updating due to addition of slang and foreign terms.
- **500s:** 3–5 years. Science works must be weeded more frequently because of advancements in the fields, especially astronomy and energy.
- **600s:** 3–5 years. Books on health and medicine, technology and industry, and travel need to be evaluated; popular books like cookbooks and pet care should be checked for wear.
- **700s:** 7–10 years. Art books do not become dated, so weed for duplications or lack of circulation; look for wear and tear and need for repair or additional titles in popular topics like drawing, music, film and television, sports, and hobbies.
- **800s:** 10 years. Literary works need weeding only for unused duplicates or damaged and worn books.
- **900s:** 5–7 years. Weed geography and travel books as this information becomes inaccurate; weed historical books based on usage and curricular needs.

- **Biographies:** 5–7 years. Notable and historical figures should be kept, but pop culture biographies should be weeded sooner; watch for circulation trends.
- **Fiction:** 5 years. Circulation trends dictate weeding of fiction, so once-popular titles can be reduced to one copy or weeded altogether when no longer sought by library users; make decisions on classics based on student interest or curricular need.

When Should You Weed?

Weeding should be done throughout the year and in small sections. Schedule it on your calendar so that you can devote time for this important task periodically; if not, you will find yourself spending whole days doing a massive amount of weeding, which makes for a frustrating and negative experience. Even if you block off just 30 minutes per week for weeding, you will end up spending about 20 hours for the task by the end of the year. If your school participates in statewide standardized testing and you are not assigned to assist with the process, take advantage of that time to do some weeding. Inventory is also a great time to weed books—as you pull a book off the shelf to scan it, you can make a decision of whether to keep the book or weed it. You should seriously consider inviting your teachers, content specialists, and department or grade-level chairs to come in and help you weed their particular area of specialty. They know their curriculum and can tell you which items are of little or no use and what topics are missing and should be ordered.

How Do You Weed?

You might weed books individually, in small groups, or in massive piles. Once you have pulled items from the shelf for removal from the collection, be sure to complete the following tasks (find out exact procedures for your library from the appropriate school or district personnel):

- Remove any listing of the item from the catalog, whether in a computer system or on cards. In a computer system, you might temporarily mark the item as withdrawn rather than deleting the record; this keeps you and library users from searching for an item that is supposed to be there but cannot be found.
- Stamp or write "discard" or "withdrawn" on the book, especially over the barcode label, the cover, the title page, and any reference to your school.
- Keep a record of withdrawn materials, even if just a running count of how many have been withdrawn. Automated systems allow you to maintain the record as "withdrawn" and easily generate a tally or listing at the end of the year.
- Dispose of the item in the manner outlined by your school or district. Some stipulate that you send the item to a district warehouse or storage area, destroy the item, recycle it, or discard it.

Note: Most districts will not allow you to sell weeded materials. Also note that items weeded for inaccurate and outdated information or questionable content should not be sent to a classroom as the purpose for weeding them was to remove them from student use.

Inventory: Why Do It?

Inventory helps you keep track of the materials in the library. As careful as you may be about circulation and security, you are bound to lose some items before the year is complete. Inventory helps you find what items were stolen, given out but not properly checked out, returned but not properly checked in, or removed but not properly withdrawn. You may also find lost items that have been returned and even items that don't belong to your library (yes, it happens). Doing inventory gets your hands on the collection and allows you the opportunity to do a little weeding. The inventory report gives you information that can help you determine which items need to be replaced next year or monitored more closely.

When to Inventory

The time most commonly chosen for inventory is the end of the year since all materials are due by then and the shelves have probably been put into order. Also, students are usually not rummaging through the collection at this time since circulation likely ended. However, you can also do inventory at the beginning of the year before students are settled into class and student accounts are loaded into your system. This is also a good time since the library probably was not used during the summer. If you close the library for a period before winter holidays (during final exams, for example), you might consider doing inventory then. Automated catalogs make inventory relatively fast and easy, so choose the time that works best for you.

Procedures for Conducting an Inventory

If you are on a manual system, you will need to first read the shelves to make sure all materials are in the correct order. Then, take a shelf list drawer to the appropriate area and begin comparing cards to books. Have a way to mark discrepancies (with a pencil or a sticky note). Once all materials have been checked, cards can be pulled and a report typed. Save cards for next year's inventory so you can determine if the items are truly gone. If an item was missing last year and is still missing this year, consider withdrawing it from the collection.

With automated systems, inventory is simple.

- Read the shelves and place items in correct order. This is not as important with automated systems as the system will usually notify you if the item is out of order when it is scanned.

- Connect a scanner to a portable computer (a computer on a wheeled cart or a laptop computer will work, for example) or use a handheld, wireless scanner or scanning device that stores barcode numbers for upload.

- Log in to your automation system and make sure inventory mode is enabled on the automation software.

- Move from item to item, shelf to shelf, scanning the barcode on each item as you go. Equipment and AV materials can be scanned for inventory as well.

- When all items have been scanned, the system will be able to generate reports and lists of missing items (see Figure 9-1).

When done, have the automated system generate a list of missing items to check against the past year's missing list. This list will also be compared against missing items from next year. As with the manual system, you may wish to withdraw items missing for more than one year.

Figure 9-1. Sample Inventory Report Screen

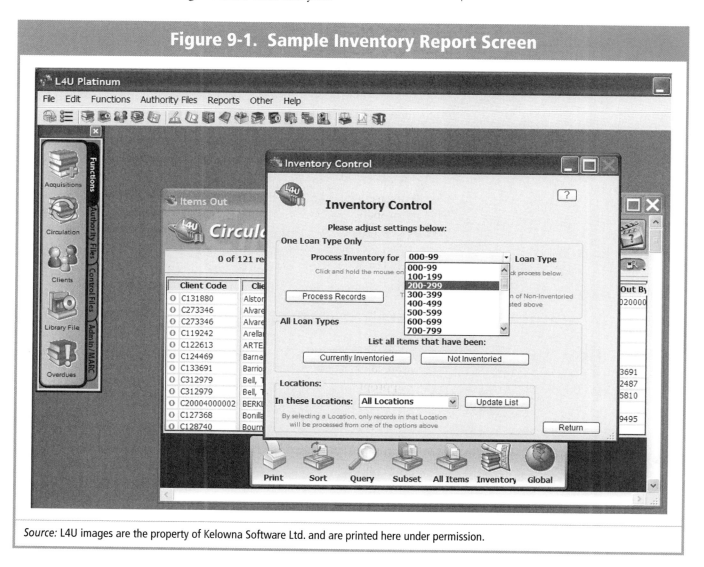

Source: L4U images are the property of Kelowna Software Ltd. and are printed here under permission.

Library Media Specialist as Information Specialist

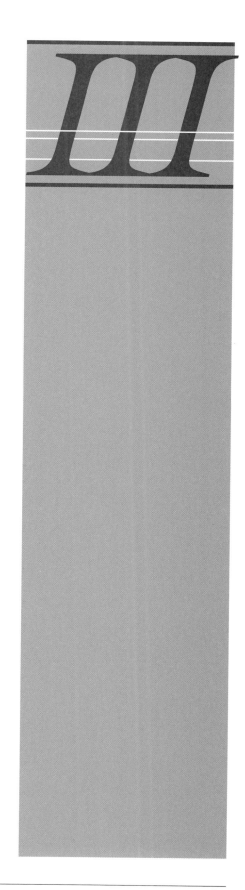

In many school districts, library schools, and professional organizations, the job title of *librarian* is being changed to better represent this very important role; in many circles, you would likely be called a "school library information specialist" or something similar. You have the responsibility and honor of being the person who can connect the school's community of users with the information they need when they need it. Have you ever walked into a library and seen tax forms in the spring, public transportation route maps, or lists of voting locations during an election? Did you know that during times of disaster in our history (like 9/11 and Hurricane Katrina), libraries and librarians became centers of emergency information and contact for the people in their communities? It is a natural reaction for librarians to take on these tasks and roles because of their daily work with information access and retrieval.

Think of yourself as a hub. A computer hub acts as a channel through which information flows from one place to another (e.g., from a network connection to an individual computer), so, too, do you act as a channel through which information flows from one place (e.g., books or databases) to another (e.g., an individual library user). Thinking of yourself this way sort of makes you feel like a superhero, doesn't it?

It is your mission (one of many, actually) to ensure that if someone has an information need, he or she can obtain the information without barriers or too much difficulty. Being in a school library puts an interesting slant on this mission because you are working with minors whose parents might not want them accessing certain information, and you are also evaluating information for appropriateness to the age level of your clientele. You must juggle these considerations with the right of intellectual freedom—the right to seek and receive information that represents a variety of viewpoints (for more details see www.ala.org/ala/oif). Your students might want to learn about Christianity or witchcraft, and they may want to find out about abstinence, birth control, or abortion. Intellectual freedom and information access is a difficult issue at the school library level because of maturity level and the ability to process and evaluate the information obtained. The best way to strike a balance is to honor children's first amendment rights by providing access to a wide variety of information that is appropriate for their age and teaching students how to locate and use information.

Information Literacy Standards for Student Learning, a guidebook for creating a solid and successful school library program, lists nine information literacy standards for student learning; the standards became the national guide for school librarians, describing the importance of information and a student's ability to find and use it effectively and ethically to gain and generate knowledge.

- STANDARD 1: The student who is information literate accesses information efficiently and effectively.
- STANDARD 2: The student who is information literate evaluates information critically and competently.
- STANDARD 3: The student who is information literate uses information accurately and creatively.
- STANDARD 4: The student who is an independent learner is information literate and pursues information related to personal interests.
- STANDARD 5: The student who is an independent learner is information literate and appreciates literature and other creative expressions of information.
- STANDARD 6: The student who is an independent learner is information literate and strives for excellence in information seeking and knowledge generation.
- STANDARD 7: The student who contributes positively to the learning community and to society is information literate and recognizes the importance of information to a democratic society.
- STANDARD 8: The student who contributes positively to the learning community and to society is information literate and practices ethical behavior in regard to information and information technology.
- STANDARD 9: The student who contributes positively to the learning community and to society is information literate and participates effectively in groups to pursue and generate information (American Library Association, 1998: 8–9).

These standards were updated by American Association of School Librarians/American Library Association and released as *Standards for the 21st-Century Learner*, focusing on student success. Read over these standards, because they will help shape decisions you will make in regard to providing information resources and services to your patrons. The overarching standards state that learners use skills, resources, and tools to do the following:

- Inquire, think critically, and gain knowledge.

- Draw conclusions, make informed decisions, apply knowledge to new situations, and create new knowledge.

- Share knowledge and participate ethically and productively as members of our democratic society.

- Pursue personal and aesthetic growth (American Association of School Librarians, 2007).

Under each broad standard are listed skills, dispositions in action, responsibilities, and self-assessment strategies; these outline specifically the abilities, beliefs, behaviors, and reflections that a successful twenty-first-century learner demonstrates.

You will play a major role in helping the students in your school achieve success as twenty-first-century learners and information users. There are several ways you provide information services and accomplish the information specialist aspect of your job: acquiring and logically arranging books, evaluating and acquiring useful electronic resources, providing easy access to a variety of resources, helping patrons determine their information needs, and teaching patrons how to assess and use the information they find.

References

American Association of School Librarians. 2007. *Standards for the 21st-Century Learner*. Chicago: American Library Association. Available: http://www.ala .org/ala/mgrps/divs/aasl/aaslproftools/learningstandards/AASL_Learning_ Standards_2007.pdf.

American Library Association. 1998. *Information Literacy Standards for Student Learning*. Chicago: American Library Association. Available: http://www .ala.org/ala/mgrps/divs/aasl/aaslproftools/informationpower/Information LiteracyStandards_final.pdf.

Selecting Books and Other Materials

Despite all of the other things you do, as a librarian you are most often associated with the "stuff" around you. You want to do a good job making sure the materials housed in your library are high-quality resources that are useful to your school community. The formal name for selecting books and other materials for purchase is *collection development*.

In Chapter 16 you will read about the importance of becoming familiar with the school's curriculum; you will be happy you did when it comes time for selecting resources for purchase. That being said, you also want to make sure the collection contains a variety of information that is valuable both for academic purposes and for leisure reading and personal research. Just as a school library that contained only fun fiction would be underutilized in the school, so would a library that had only books that fit into the curriculum. By balancing your collection with books for research and pleasure reading, you will ensure that the library is a place that students and teachers can frequent for their information and literacy needs.

Figuring Out What Materials You Need

There is no way you will ever acquire every single book that your school community might want. However, making informed choices will help you fill your shelves with a wide variety of information that will meet most of your users' information needs. The first step you'll want to take, if possible, is to perform a collection analysis. A collection analysis (also discussed in Chapter 1) will give you data about the items in the collection, including their age and the amount of materials covering different topics. Some companies will provide the service at a cost and will do all the work themselves; some book-vending companies offer a similar service online at no charge to their customers if you simply upload your data file. Either way, the information and reports generated will greatly assist you in determining gaps in your collection and areas that need to be improved with updated materials. Figure 10-1 shows a sample collection analysis generated using Follett Library Resources' Titlewave® Online Collection Analysis.

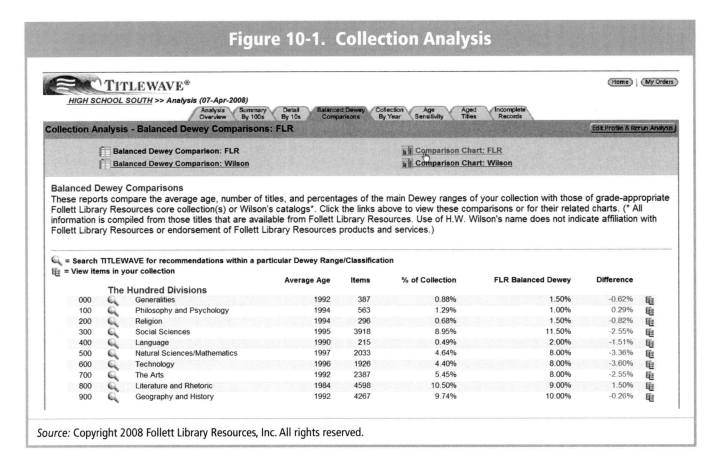

Figure 10-1. Collection Analysis

Once you've run a collection analysis and have seen where the gaps and aged materials lie, find out if it is worth updating these areas. You may have only a few materials in the sections on animal husbandry and agriculture, but if your school is in the city and there are no farms nearby or agricultural science classes in your building, you probably don't need to improve that part of the collection. If you have only one book about snakes but several of your students have pet snakes and the biology classes include a unit on reptiles, you probably should purchase more materials in that area. Getting a feel for students' interests will help you with material selection—if you don't seek the information they will gladly volunteer it with phrases like, "Why don't you ever have any books about ___?". You will also want to talk to content or grade-level specialists, department chairs, and teachers since they can provide you with valuable information about what they teach and materials they need and will use in their classrooms. Ask the teachers and administrators in your school for a list of materials that they would like. If they don't have a list, make it easy for them to recommend a book for purchase by providing a short form or slip that teachers and students can complete and drop in a suggestion box for purchases. If your library has a Web page on the school Web site, make your suggestion for purchase form available online also.

As the year goes on and you get to know your collection and your school community, you will find it easier to determine where your money should go. Creating a collection that contains materials your users want and need will help you build a school library that is utilized and valued.

Reviews (for Books and Other Materials)

Another great resource to help you choose books and other materials (e.g., audiovisuals and equipment) is professional reviews. Your district or school should have in place a selection policy that outlines how materials are selected for inclusion in the library (see Chapter 5); the policy should mention that the librarian uses professional review sources to assist with selecting books and other materials for purchase. You cannot be familiar with every single book before you purchase it, so you must rely on the professional judgment of others to determine whether or not you should consider materials for purchase.

Luckily, there are many review sources available to librarians (see Part VII). Most school librarians use *School Library Journal* and *Booklist* as review sources, but several others are available. These periodicals provide reviews of newly released books and other materials and are written by professionals, many written by librarians. Browsing the reviews each month will give you a good idea of new titles you may want to consider for your next order. Jot down titles and authors, scan or copy the review, and put the information in a folder. Keep in mind that, regardless of how many other things you do during the day, you will encounter some issue each day that is related to collection development, even if it is just that you walk by a shelf and notice that books on a particular subject are falling apart. Keeping an ongoing list of books that you want to purchase (based on faculty and student requests, collection analysis, and reviews) will make your job much easier when it comes time to actually put your order together.

Other Materials—The Vertical File

Librarians have used the term "vertical file" to mean a collection of materials kept in a filing cabinet and of interest to users of that library. In school libraries, these materials are sometimes not kept in a filing cabinet but are shelved or displayed in the general library area. Consider storing them electronically if space is a problem; the concept, however, is the same. Items you might order or collect are pamphlets, photos and illustrations, magazine or newspaper clippings, catalogs, etc.—items that are of interest and need to your school population. For example, a high school librarian may request pamphlets from universities, technical schools, and the armed forces, and these pamphlets might be displayed in the career and college area. Many of these types of materials are available free of charge. A few things to remember:

- Find out what your users need and then look for materials.
- Don't get overzealous and end up with useless clutter.
- Determine if these items will be used in the library only, checked out and returned, or simply given away if you have many copies.

- If items will be kept for in-library use or checkout, create records in the catalog and decide the best method for checkout.
- Monitor the use of these items; if they aren't used, get rid of them.
- Weed out old materials and replace them frequently to avoid incorrect information.

Ordering and Processing Books and Other Materials

Ordering Books

Selecting and then ordering books and getting them onto the shelves of your library is a major task. Don't worry—you can do this. As frightening as it may seem to select and order hundreds or thousands of dollars' worth of books or other materials for your library, it is a manageable task. The same principles apply as if you were spending your own money shopping online with a credit card: buy what you need at the best price available, with fast, reliable shipping.

You will first need to determine where you will purchase books. Find out if your school or district has a list of approved or committed vendors. If so, you are limited to ordering from those vendors. If not, shop around, looking for the best prices and reliable service. You can locate and order books from publishers, from bookstores, and from catalogs. You can often get the best prices if you use a jobber or vendor—a wholesaler who stocks books and sells them to libraries at a discount. In addition to lower prices, jobbers offer one-stop shopping rather than purchasing individual books from individual publishers; the larger vendors even offer processing on materials, including barcoding, labeling, and MARC record creation. If you have limited time or staff to process books, this can be a valuable service that is usually available at a reasonable price.

Although you can fill in catalog order forms by hand or have vendors visit your school and create orders for you, you can now easily complete orders online with most large book vendors. Several vendors even allow you to create an online account and establish lists to which you can add, delete, and update items as often as you like, which means your ongoing list of wanted materials can all be done electronically and on the site of the vendor from which you will make the purchase. Online you can easily locate materials and prices, find alternate titles, search for materials by topic, read reviews, create your order, and even specify processing details. Figure 11-1 shows a sample list from Follett Library Resources' Web site (www.titlewave .com). It would be worthwhile for you to find approved vendors with

Figure 11-1. Vendor Online Order Screen

online catalogs and ordering and then try them out to discover which vendors will make the ordering process fast, simple, and painless.

In addition to a list of what books you are ordering, the vendor will probably ask you for additional information to go with some processing and cataloging options available to you. If you can spare the minimal additional cost, these options will make adding the books to your collection a much easier task; it allows the vendor to do most of the preparation work for you before the books even arrive at your school. If you pay the vendor to do some of the processing, you will need to complete a processing specifications sheet (see Figure 11-2). These specifications tell the vendor how you label and classify books in your library so that the vendor can create labels and MARC records appropriately. Some other options available during ordering are the following:

- Barcode labels: This option prevents you from needing to create and print your own labels. You can also have the vendor attach the labels to your books and place a protective film over them. When deciding where to have the labels placed, consider such factors as what will be covered by the label (title, cover art, etc.) and how easily you can get to the label to scan it during inventory. For example, inside cover placement means that during inventory you have to remove every book from the shelf and open the cover in order to scan the label; this is not recommended.

- Spine label: This label shows the call number and helps with shelf placement. You will need to decide how far you want the label to be placed from the bottom of the book. These labels are also covered with a protective film.

- Theft detection: The vendor can place the theft detection/security patch or strip in the book for you. You must know which alarm system is installed in your library and the type of theft detection strip or patch that is used.

- Date-due card and pocket: If you do not keep a surplus of these items in your library, you can have the vendor send them or even attach them for you. Having these preattached will cost extra, so you will save money by simply attaching these yourself. Often, these can be personalized with the name of your school.

- Shelf list card: If you still maintain a shelf list of cards, you can have the vendor send completed cards for you to simply add to your catalog; however, many libraries with electronic systems are no longer maintaining a card shelf list.

- Electronic catalog records: A MARC (machine-readable cataloging) record is a standard-format digital record of bibliographic information used to describe materials. The information is divided into fields and subfields that specify the type of information, such as title, author, publisher, etc. MARC was developed by the Library of Congress to aid in the creation and sharing of bibliographic records between library catalogs. Most vendors will make available to you MARC records for the items you order. These can be sent to you on a CD-ROM, diskette, or by e-mail. To add the items to your collection, you simply download the records into your automated system. Information on creating or obtaining MARC records yourself can be found later in this chapter.

- Shelf-ready packing: Some vendors will box large orders in numerical and/or alphabetical order as they would be placed on your shelves, allowing you to simply open the boxes and shelve the books without sorting.

If a general processing specifications document is not already available in your school library, it will save you time and confusion if you create one for future reference. You can refer to it when completing forms and can even give it to some vendors who may not have their own specifications form. A sample is shown in Figure 11-3.

Some notes about finalizing your order: Rather than simply submitting your order online, you will most likely need to complete a purchase request and submit it to your purchasing department in order to have the order approved and sent. It is recommended that you order more than what you want to spend (approximately 30% more) in case some books are not available or out of print. On your purchase request, make a notation of "Do Not Exceed" along with the amount you wish to spend; this will tell the vendor to fill as much of the order as possible without going over the amount that you budgeted. If you specify "Do Not Exceed," be sure to prioritize the

Figure 11-2. Processing Specifications Sheet (from Vendor)

Processing Specifications

(please place an "x" to indicate selection and submit this form with your order)

Use Subject Headings:

[ ] Sears
[ ] Library of Congress

Fiction:

[ ] F + first 3 letters of author's last name
[ ] FIC + first 3 letters of author's last name
[ ] classification # + first 2 letters of author's last name
[ ] classification # + author's full last name

Easy Fiction:

[ ] E + first 3 letters of author's last name
[ ] E + first 2 letters of author's last name
[ ] first 3 letters of author's last name
[ ] same as fiction

Individual Biography:

[ ] B + first 3 letters of subject's last name
[ ] B + subject's full last name
[ ] 921 + first 3 letters of subject's last name

Collective Biography:

[ ] 920 + first 3 letters of author's last name
[ ] 920 + author's full last name
[ ] BC + first 3 letters of author's last name

Story Collection:

[ ] 808.8 + first 3 letters of author's last name
[ ] SC + first 3 letters of author's last name
[ ] SC + first 2 letters of author's last name
[ ] same as fiction

Reference:

[ ] R + classification #
[ ] REF + classification #
[ ] R + classification # + first 3 letters of author's last name
[ ] REF + classification # + first 3 letters of author's last name

Foreign Language:

[ ] classification #
[ ] classification # + first 3 letters of author's last name
[ ] language code + classification #
[ ] language code + first 3 letters of author's last name
[ ] language code + classification # + first 3 letters of author's last name

Professional:

[ ] P + classification #
[ ] PRO + classification #
[ ] P + classification # + first 3 letters of author's last name
[ ] PRO + classification # + first 3 letters of author's last name

Classifications (for nonfiction):

Carry out decimal to _____ places

[ ] classification # + first 3 letters of author's last name
[ ] classification # + first 2 letters of author's last name
[ ] classification # + author's full last name

* For more options not listed, please call prior to placing order.

books in your order so that the vendor will fill the higher priority items first and will fill the remaining books only if the price limit allows.

Print or photocopy your list of books and include them with the request, making a notation of "Books per Attached List" rather than typing in every title and price. Be sure you've included processing and shipping costs, if applicable. Also, make sure to keep a copy of the full order for your records. Find out the correct ordering procedure from your school secretary or district purchasing department to avoid mistakes. Make a note of any request numbers or purchase order numbers that are generated so that you can refer to them if there is a problem with the order.

Figure 11-3. General Processing Specifications Sheet

Processing Information for:
South HS, Texas ISD

—Spine labels + protectors, attached

—MARC records <USMARC (852 holdings)>:
* preferred—by e-mail to: Marco.Zannier@myschool.net
or data CD
Library software: L4U Platinum

—Barcodes + protectors, attached (upper left on front of book, vertical, reading up)
Code 3 of 9/NO check digit
13-digit barcode
STARTING BAR CODE NUMBER: 3000200800100

—Cataloging classification options (ALL CAPITALIZED)
Individual Biography: B + entire last name
Collective Biography: 920 + 3 letters
Nonfiction: Dewey (3 places after decimal) + 3 letters
Reference: R + 3 letters
Story Collections: SC + 3 letters
Easy/Everybody: E + 3 letters
Fiction: F + 3 letters

—NO AR LABEL

—Name to appear on barcodes:
SOUTH HIGH SCHOOL

When the Books Arrive at Your Door (Processing)

The first thing you'll want to do when you receive the order is to find the packing slip or invoice and the copy of your original order list (you did keep a copy, didn't you?); unpack the books and match them against the lists. If you find discrepancies, contact the vendor or your purchasing department—this depends on the procedural protocols for your school. Also be on the lookout for defective or damaged books. File the packing slip or invoice or copies of them with the copies of your order list and purchase order. If your purchasing department requires you to send them a receiving slip or a signed copy of the packing slip, do this now before you forget. This step ensures payment for the order. Now you're ready for processing.

If you paid for the vendor to do most of the processing, you don't have much left to do. Verify the information on the MARC records and verify that any duplicates to books in your collection have the same call number so they are shelved together. Be sure that duplicate copies are marked as copy 2, copy 3, etc. to distinguish them. If you are still using shelf list cards, add the vendor name, date, price, and purchase order number to the cards. Check to see if all labels are correctly and securely attached. Stamp your school name in the books, add pockets or date due cards as needed, and cover the book jackets with plastic if necessary. The books are ready for the shelves.

If you are processing the books yourself, here are some steps:

- Create MARC records or shelf list cards. The Library of Congress Web site can help with MARC record creation (http://catalog.loc .gov/). Perform a basic search for the book/material, select the record you want, and then click the "MARC tags" tab. The MARC record can be copied or downloaded (select MARC format). Once copied or downloaded, the record can be loaded into your automation system's catalog. Be sure to include purchase information, such as vendor, price, etc. Library automation systems now make it simple to create records by just filling in blanks, like title, author's name, etc.; this topic is covered in Chapter 12. Software is also available to help you with record creation, and some is free (www.loc.gov/marc/marctools.html). For help with Dewey classification and selection of subject headings, see Chapter 12.

- Create barcodes and spine labels and attach them. Covering them with a clear adhesive film will protect them from wear and tear.

- Stamp your school's name in the book. Other than the inside front and/or back cover, you might want to stamp the side of the book where the pages meet when the book is closed or a blank space on a random page in the book. You should use the same page number in all books so the stamp is easy to locate. This helps identify ownership if the cover is removed or the stamp is covered, erased, or damaged.

- Add any security patches or strips your library uses.

- Cover dust jackets to protect them.

- Attach a pocket and a date due card.

Audiovisuals

Ordering audiovisual (AV) materials is very similar to ordering books. Guidelines are probably stricter and fewer vendors available to you in this case, so be sure to find out any regulations your school or district has regarding AV and equipment purchases. When selecting AV, rely heavily on input from specialists, department chairs, and teachers, since these materials tend to be a little more costly than books and you don't want to order items that won't be used. Check reviews to make sure the materials are age-appropriate, especially videos. When processing AV materials, check for manufacturer damage (like scratches on DVDs) and make sure they work. Write your school name in permanent marker directly on the materials if possible (this works well with CDs, videocassettes, and DVDs).

Equipment

Again, find out what regulations your school or district has for ordering equipment and be sure to use approved or committed vendors. When selecting equipment, make sure it is:

- useful, not just flashy;

- cost-effective—purchase it only if it is worth buying (if some other equipment you already own can do the job, skip the expense);

- portable—if it will be circulated and move from room to room;

- well-built and sturdy—remember that you are in a school, not a museum;

- fairly easy to operate—the faculty does not have abundant time to read manuals or go through training;

- easy to maintain—ensure parts, bulbs, cartridges, etc., are easily available; and

- easy to repair—will it be "in the shop" too much to be useful?

When processing equipment, you should first make sure it is not damaged. Test it to make sure it works properly and as advertised. Mark the equipment with the school's name (use permanent marker) and, if it is the procedure, with a school or district identification tag. If you will be scanning the equipment for circulation, create barcodes; if you are using a manual system, create a spreadsheet on which you can log circulation. Keep any manuals, warranty information, and other paperwork filed somewhere safe. You may file it with the ordering paperwork or you might keep a filing cabinet drawer that houses only this type of paperwork.

Organizing and Arranging Books

If you choose to order books without preprocessing and cataloging, you or a library staff member will need to process and catalog (classify by subject) the books yourself. Although you will be able to find cataloging information online (MARC records) from sources like the Library of Congress, it will help you to know a little about how the Dewey Decimal classification system organizes books. The Dewey Decimal system is preferred in school libraries because of ease of use. Knowing a little about it will help you gain a better understanding of how your library is arranged and why books are located in the places they are. If you will be doing your own cataloging and determining the appropriate call numbers for your newly acquired books, you will need to purchase the *Dewey Decimal Classification and Relative Index* (the abridged, one-volume version is available for under $100; Dewey et al., 2004). This chapter covers the basics of the classification system to give you a general overview of how it's organized and also discusses selection of subject headings that will help library users locate books in the electronic catalog.

How the Dewey Decimal Classification System Works

The Dewey Decimal classification system, developed by librarian and ALA founding member Melvil Dewey in the late 1800s, places topics or subjects into categories and subcategories, and subcategories of subcategories. At the time Dewey developed it, the system was intended to cover all knowledge—every possible topic. Much has changed in the world since that time, and new subjects and discoveries are "crowded" into the system, requiring lengthy subdivisions in many of the categories. The overarching ten categories are:

000–099	General Works
100–199	Philosophy
200–299	Religion
300–399	Social Science and Folklore
400–499	Language

IN THIS CHAPTER:

✔ How the Dewey Decimal Classification System Works

✔ Assigning Subject Headings

✔ Cataloging a Book

✔ Placement on Shelves

✔ Organizing and Arranging Audiovisuals

500–599	Math and Natural Science
600–699	Applied Science and Technology
700–799	Art and Recreation
800–899	Literature
900–999	History and Geography

Each overarching category is then divided into ten subcategories (see Figure 12-1), which are each then further divided into subcategories and decimals. Every book you purchase can be categorized and assigned a number with decimals, and this number denotes very specifically the subject of the book.

For ease of location, libraries, especially school libraries, have created other identifying codes that are not part of the Dewey classification system but are easily identifiable by library users. These codes allow you to further label or even pull parts of the collection out of the areas arranged by numerical classification, creating sections of the library with specific types of materials. Some of the more common codes used in school libraries are:

B	Biography
CC	College and Career
E	Easy or Everyone (picture books, children's books)
F or Fic	Fiction
GN	Graphic Novel
PRO	Professional (education books, for faculty)
R or Ref	Reference
SC or SS	Story Collection (Short Stories)
AV	Audiovisuals (further divided: CDR, DVD, VC, etc.)

Assigning Subject Headings

Determining the Dewey classification places the book in the numerical sequence of the system, thus assigning it a place on the shelf. However, the book must still be assigned a subject heading (or more, if warranted) so that library users can locate the book in the electronic card catalog. You should assign the subject heading that best describes the whole book using either subject headings that already exist in your catalog for other books on the same topic or using a standard source to determine a subject heading. Sources for subject headings include the *Sears List of Subject Headings* (Miller and Goodsell, 2007) or the *Library of Congress Subject Headings* (Library of Congress, 2007). An electronic catalog will have an authority file that will help keep the subject headings consistent. Select enough subject headings to adequately describe the book so your users can find it in the electronic card catalog.

Cataloging a Book

Each book needs to have a record in the electronic catalog so that library users can find the book. The process of creating this record is called *cataloging*. As noted in Chapter 11, you can locate the MARC record for a book online

Figure 12-1. Dewey Classification by Tens

000	Knowledge	300	Sociology	600	Technology
010	Bibliographies	310	General statistics	610	Medical science
020	Library/Info. science	320	Political science	620	Engineering
030	Fact books, Encycl.	330	Economics	630	Agriculture
040	Unassigned	340	Law	640	Home economics
050	Serials	350	Public admin.	650	Management, PR
060	Organizations	360	Social services	660	Chemical engineering
070	Media, Journalism	370	Education	670	Manufacturing
080	General collection	380	Commerce	680	Specific manufactur.
090	Rare books	390	Customs, Folklore	690	Buildings
100	Philosophy	400	Language	700	Fine arts
110	Metaphysics	410	Linguistics	710	Civic/landscape art
120	Epistemology	420	English (& related)	720	Architecture
130	Paranormal	430	German (& related)	730	Plastic arts, Sculpting
140	Schools of thought	440	French (& related)	740	Drawing
150	Psychology	450	Italian (& related)	750	Painting
160	Logic	460	Spanish (& related)	760	Graphics
170	Ethics	470	Latin, Italic	770	Photography
180	Ancient philosophy	480	Greek, Hellenic	780	Music
190	Modern philosophy	490	Other languages	790	Perform., Recreation
200	Religion	500	Natural Science	800	Literature, Rhetoric
210	Natural theology	510	Math	810	American lit.
220	The Bible	520	Astronomy	820	English lit.
230	Christian theology	530	Physics	830	Germanic lit.
240	Christian practice	540	Chemistry	840	Romance (lang.) lit.
250	Christian orders	550	Earth science	850	Italian lit.
260	Christian organization	560	Paleontology	860	Spanish lit.
270	Christian history	570	Life sci., Physiology	870	Latin, Italic lit.
280	Christian denomin.	580	Botanical science	880	Hellenic, Greek lit.
290	Other religions	590	Zoological science	890	Other lang. lit.

900	World history	950	Asia: history and geography
910	Geography, Travel	960	Africa: history and geography
920	Biography, Genealogy, Insignia	970	N. America: history and geography
930	Ancient world history	980	S. America: history and geography
940	Europe: history and geography	990	Other areas: history and geography

and then import it into your electronic system so that you can begin with all of the basic information (author, title, etc.); however, you will still need to check to be sure that the Dewey number and subject heading(s) assigned to the MARC record fit into your collection. Earlier books on the same subject may have been assigned a different classification number or subject, and you may need to make changes to the MARC record.

If you are cataloging "from scratch," your electronic system will provide a template for you to input the key information to create the record for a book. See Figure 12-2 for an example of a record template. The basic information that the template will prompt you for (called "fields") will include the following:

- Author(s): Full name of the author(s)
- Title: Full title of the book
- Description:.The physical information about the book—number of pages, illustrations, sometimes even the size of the book
- Bibliographics: Name of publisher, place of publication, date of publication, ISBN
- Call number: The Dewey classification number that you have chosen, or a letter assignment
- Subjects: The subject headings you have selected, matching them to preexisting subject headings if already in the system
- Added fields: This might include series information, an added title, or other information (e.g., an illustrator)

Note: Each electronic system will have its own template for entering your cataloging information; the previous information is an introduction of what to anticipate when doing your own cataloging versus purchasing precatalogued books from a book jobber.

Placement on Shelves

Books are arranged on the shelves according to the classification code or call number. Books classified using the Dewey Decimal system are arranged first in numerical order, by whole number and decimals, and then alphabetically, by the author's last name, often labeled by the first letter or the first three letters of the last name. For example:

641	641.2	641.4	641.43	641.43	641.44
JAQ	CLE	BRI	FRA	LEM	HON

Books classified by the Dewey Decimal system but housed in separate sections, such as professional or reference books, are still arranged numerically within that section. Books classified outside of the Dewey system using the easier identifying codes such as those listed above are arranged alphabetically within their section. Fiction, for example, is done this way:

F	F	F	F	F	F
AAR	ASH	BLA	BLU	BUR	CAN

Figure 12-2. Record Template

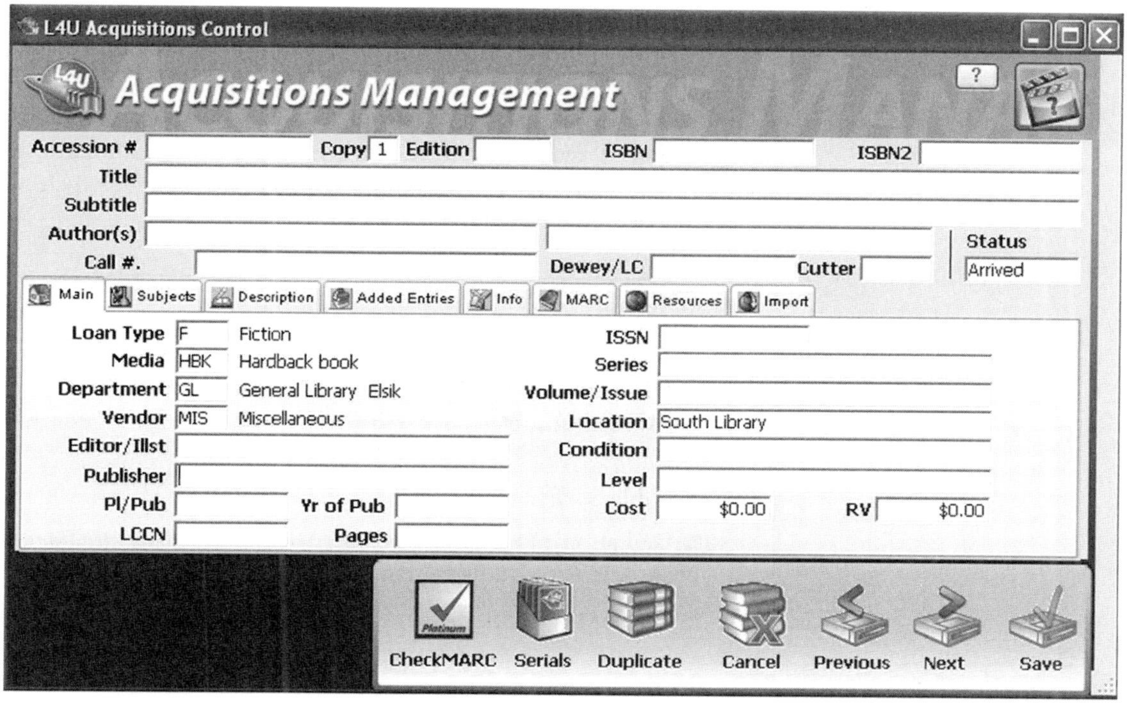

Source: L4U images are the property of Kelowna Software Ltd. and are printed here under permission.

Shelve these types of books carefully, because you must look beyond the letters on the spine label for correct placement. There may be several authors with the same identifying letters (for example, WIN would be the letters for the last names Winchester, Winfrey, Winkler, Winston, and Winters). All books by the same author should be shelved together and then alphabetically by book title.

Organizing and Arranging Audiovisuals

Different schools of thought exist as to how audiovisuals should be shelved. One school believes that all items should be intershelved, placing together all materials about the same topic despite format; this method causes problems with efficient use of space and type of shelving used because audiovisuals with different formats come in different sizes. Another school of thought believes that materials of the same format should be shelved together and then arranged by Dewey Classification number; this method requires separate areas with different shelves and plenty of space. The most widely used method in school libraries is the creation of an AV room or AV area in which all AV/non-print materials are shelved together and arranged by Dewey Classification number; although it doesn't keep all materials on the same topic together, this method allows for easy browsing and location of the materials by the faculty and makes it easy for you to monitor the materials.

Audiovisual materials will also be cataloged into your electronic system. While some information will remain the same for input, the overall codes and fields will differ slightly from cataloging books. For example, rather than number of pages, for an audiovisual, your system might prompt you for running time if the AV is a videotape or DVD. Become familiar with your system and the fields that are required for cataloging an AV item so that you are prepared to input information for each field when prompted by your electronic system.

References

Dewey, Melvil, Joan S. Mitchell, Julianne Beall, Giles Martin, Winton E. Matthews, and Gregory R. New. 2004. *Dewey Decimal Classification and Relative Index*, 14th edition. Dublin, OH: OCLC Online Computer Library Center.

Library of Congress. 2007. *Library of Congress Subject Headings*, 30th edition. Washington, DC: Library of Congress.

Miller, Joseph, and Joan Goodsell. 2007. *Sears List of Subject Headings*, 19th edition. Bronx, NY: H. W. Wilson Company.

Selecting Databases and Web Sites

Although you will still find plenty of magazines in school libraries, you will probably see students looking at them as leisure reading rather than using them for research purposes. You will also probably not see tables full of students taking notes from print encyclopedias. Constant advancements in technology and the increased sophistication of students' computer skills have made electronic periodicals and databases the new research resources. Print indexes like the *Readers' Guide to Periodical Literature* disappeared as students gained the ability to type in search criteria and retrieve journal articles electronically within a matter of seconds. In most school and public libraries, you will see students using computers for research and searching in databases to find the information they need. If your budget allows it, add database subscriptions to the list of valuable services and materials your library offers to your school community.

Why Databases?

Books, as always, have valuable information in them that can be used by your students for research. You should continue to promote and educate students about the use of print resources in your library. Practically speaking, however, there are some limitations to print resources for research:

- You have a limited number of books on a specific topic.
- You have outdated materials.
- Even current-year print materials don't include today's news.
- Pinpointing needed information within a book takes time.
- Price—the cost of about 50 reference books, which can be used by about 50 students—equals the cost of a database subscription, which can be used by the entire student body and faculty at the same time.
- Quality—the information in databases is professionally collected, edited, and reviewed for accuracy. As much as students surf the

Web, they are not selective about where they get their information; databases give them reliable information while avoiding random Internet searching.

How to Obtain Databases

If you are in a school district, check with the district library or technology coordinator to see if he or she already subscribes to some databases for the whole district to use; these databases would be paid for by the district budget. Your district may also have agreements or commitments with certain database vendors that will give you a discounted subscription price. Check with your state library association, too, as your state may offer discounts on selected databases. Database subscription vendors set up booths at your state library association's annual conference, and you can get information and discounts by talking to them at these meetings. Your local public library might have databases that your students can use if they have a library card; you can add links to those databases on your school's Web site, and students can then simply enter their library card number or password.

As you begin to look for databases to which you might possibly subscribe, you will notice that there is quite a variety to choose from. Databases contain current magazine and journal articles, encyclopedias, medical and health information, historical newspaper articles, current events essays, maps and photos, career information, biographies, and much more. Determine what your faculty and students need (by being familiar with curriculum, finding gaps in the collection, and paying attention to research requests) and base your purchase decisions on what will best serve the needs of your school community.

Most database subscription vendors will give you a free trial period so you can use the database and determine if it is right for your school. If they don't offer it, ask them for it—and insist on it. Databases are expensive, so you don't want to end up with one that is a lemon or is something your students won't use. Ask your teachers to come to the library and test the database themselves and get feedback from them. If you can get a student or two to test it, do so. Doing plenty of on-site evaluation will help you make the right choice.

Promoting Database Use

Once you acquire a database or two, you will need to convince others to use these resources. Start by placing links to the databases on your library's Web site so your school community can easily access the databases. You will be given a username and password from the vendor to give to your users so they can access the vendor's system. This ensures that only paid users can access the database. Make login information available to faculty and students via e-mail and attach labels to school computers and any other place where students can get to it. Don't publish login information on your Web site since anyone can see it there and this would be a breach of the contractual

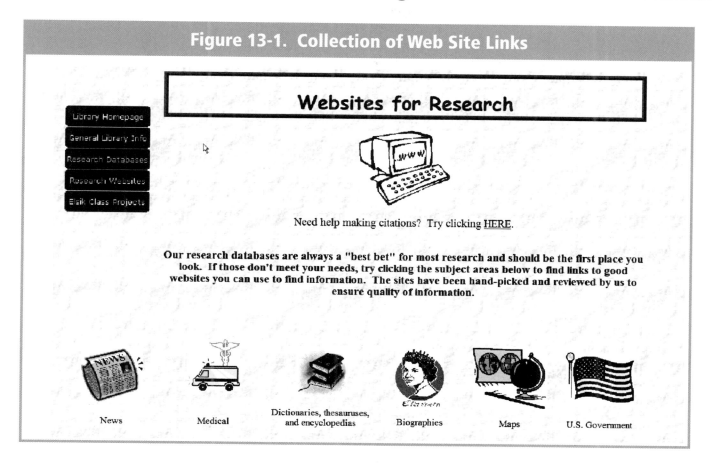

Figure 13-1. Collection of Web Site Links

limitation of users. Meet with the faculty (in content or grade level teams works well) and show them the database; tailor your presentation to their particular teaching areas so they will see how useful a tool the database can be. Offer to visit classrooms or hold training sessions in the library so that you can instruct students on use of the database. Create a brief Webcast video tutorial of how to use the database and ask teachers to take a few minutes from their schedule to show it to their class. When students come to the library to do research, direct them to the database and help them use it to find the information they need.

Web Sites

Why the sudden switch in topic to Web sites? Many students prefer to do their research searching on the Internet as a whole rather than in books or even electronic databases. Although you spent a lot of money on them and know they contain reliable information, your databases won't contain every single bit of information your students will need (see Figure 13-1). Some assignments or research topics are very specific and will require students to go outside the books and databases and use the Internet. Unfortunately, "Internet" has become a dirty word among some educators because of the vast amount of inaccurate and inappropriate content. As a librarian, you

RECOMMENDED DATABASES

Encyclopedia Britannica
http://school.eb.com
Gale
http://www.gale.cengage.com/
Grolier
http://go-passport.grolier.com/
netTrekker
http://school.nettrekker.com
Proquest
http://www.proquest.com
World Book
http://www.worldbookonline.com

might secretly be glad that your faculty and students have access to such an immense resource, so promote the educated use of this resource for personal and academic research.

Teach your students how to navigate the Web successfully. Just typing a topic into a search engine (like Google) will yield millions of results that are useless, waste time, and cause frustration. Students should decide ahead of time what type of information they need, think of reliable sources that would have that information, and then navigate to those sites. For example, if a student is doing a report on the moon, scientists who study it would have the best information; since NASA has astronomers and moon experts, a reliable site to visit would be www.nasa.gov. Without this prethinking, typing in the word "moon" on a search engine would yield over 433,000,000 hits for the student to check, most of which are not on topic or not reliable.

Teach students (and faculty) how to evaluate Web sites before using the information contained on them. Have students go through a 4-C checklist:

- Credibility—Who wrote the content on the site? Would they be knowledgeable about the subject? Are they and the information objective or biased? Is there a way to contact them for verification or clarification, or are they unreachable?

- Cause—Why is this site on the Web? Is it educational and informative, or is it trying to sell you something or some idea? Is it a .com, .gov, .edu, etc.? Is it someone's personal page or blog that presents opinions and biases rather than facts?

- Content—Is there valuable information on the site? Is it useful to you? Is there similar content available online from a better source? Is there extra "junk" on the site that is unneeded and distracting?

- Currency—Is the site maintained and updated? Is any of the information outdated? Are links on the site working or dead?

For further information on using the Internet for research purposes, see the section For More Information on Research Skills in Chapter 18.

Web Site Collections

It would be beneficial to you, the students, and the teachers if you collected URLs of quality Web sites that might be useful for research. Again, knowing the curriculum, student interests, and common research topics in your school will help you determine what sites would be most useful. Stick to the most commonly searched topics first and then add topics as needed so that you don't waste hours and hours up front locating and linking to sites that might never be used. Your URL collection does not need to be extensive— three to five sites on a topic should be enough to satisfy your students' needs. Keep a print copy of the URLs and create links or bookmarks on your library Web site or library computers so library users can simply click and get to the sites directly.

Creating Your Library's Web Site (and More)

One of the struggles of school librarians in the twenty-first century is that the library is no longer contained within four walls. You still assist students and teachers who visit the library, but your library users are reading and researching from their classrooms and home computers as well. To truly provide services to your school community, you need to meet them where they are—and often they are online. One of the best ways you can provide access to services and promote your library is by having a useful and user-friendly library Web site (see Figure 14-1 for a sample Web site). Your site can be accessed by anyone in the world, and it shows what you are doing and what you have to offer. We've mentioned your library's Web site many times thus far in this book; in this chapter, you'll learn more about creating the site and what to put on it.

The Webmaster

If possible, be the creator and master of your library's Web site. Some schools or districts have technology personnel who do all of the Web publishing for the schools; if this is the case, ask if you can meet with those personnel so that you can provide input and help design the library's page. After all, who knows better what should be on the library's page than the librarian? If you have the ability to control your page, take advantage of that opportunity. Make your site another valuable resource you offer to the school community. Plenty of software is available to help you make Web pages, and you do not even need to be familiar with HTML (hypertext markup language). Check to see if there is already some Web design software loaded onto your library computers and learn how to use it so that you can create and maintain a dynamic site that will be used.

Some Web Site Basics

If you have ever been online, you have seen good sites and bad sites. Some design tips are true to all Web sites and pages to help avoid making a bad site. Here are a few to help you get started:

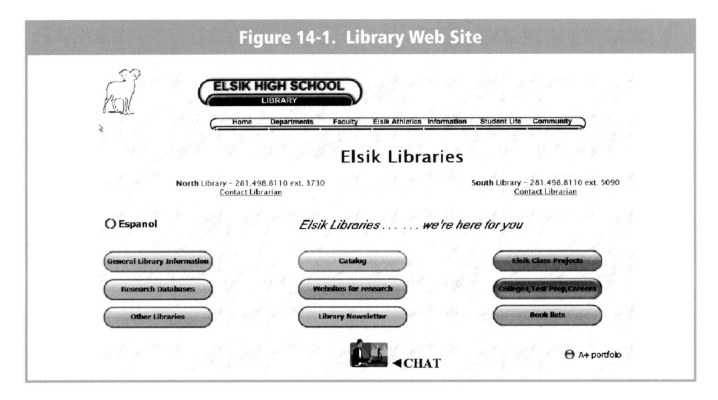

Figure 14-1. Library Web Site

- Keep the site pages neat and organized; don't have text, graphics, and links randomly thrown around.
- Use colors that work well together, do not reduce legibility, do not cause eye strain, and do not prevent those with color blindness from seeing everything on your site. Black on yellow or dark blue on white work well; limit reds and greens as they reduce visibility for people with color blindness.
- Avoid making the site too flashy; blinking lights, music, and hopping bunnies may seem cute to you, but they slow down your site and make the page a confusing mess.
- Try keeping pages screen-sized so visitors don't need to keep scrolling up and down to read the page.
- Don't make visitors click more than three times to get to whatever information or resource they need.
- Include navigation buttons so visitors can get around easily.
- Hyperlink URLs so visitors can click and go.

Figure 14-2 presents a form you can use to evaluate the content and quality of your Web site.

What to Include

The content of your site will depend on the sophistication of your Web design abilities, what resources you have available, the needs of your school

Figure 14-2. Library Web Site Evaluation Form

GOOD Web sites...

have a clean appearance
have simple, consistent navigation ("3 click" rule)
are organized
have useful, working links
are easy to read
are current and fresh (keep 'em coming back)
are tailored to user needs
get to the point
get good information to the user efficiently
are valuable tools

BAD Web sites...

have visibly confusing color schemes
are difficult to navigate
are confusing and hodge-podge
have broken links and mystery-meat buttons
have illegible text and are wordy
are outdated and seldom revised
don't consider user need or experience
are full of bells and whistles
are more style than substance
are a waste of space

10 Things to consider when designing your library's Web site:

1. Make sure it's linked from the school's home page.
2. Use consistent design elements.
3. Don't use wild color schemes, fonts, or animations.
4. Use a navigation bar.
5. space wisely, and don't make your users scroll too much.
6. "Chunk" information and develop a simple organization.
7. Minimize the number of clicks needed to get places!
8. Include details to help users determine information need (like database descriptions).
9. Design and organize based on user need and task frequency.
10. Avoid jargon/tech-speak (like "IPAC").

User needs for _____ : _____

_____

_____

Site:

	exemplary (5)	above avg. (4)	fair (3)	below avg. (2)	poor (1)
Content is relevant and useful to intended clients.					
Graphics, sound, and video enhance rather than distract.					
Navigation is smooth and simple to use.					
Information is found within 3 clicks.					
Hyperlinks work (no dead links).					
Layout is logical and not cluttered.					
Color scheme is pleasing and doesn't interfere with visibility.					
Text is easily legible and not lengthy.					
Contact information is included.					
OVERALL the page/site is attractive, useful, and user-friendly.					
	score total:		X 2 =		/100 ◄ GRADE

community, and how much time you can devote to keeping the site current. Here are some suggestions of things you might want to include:

- Library information: location, hours, policies, procedures, etc.
- Librarian information: who you are, contact number or e-mail, etc.
- Library staff information (if you have staff)
- Library news
- Library calendar and special events
- Link to the OPAC/online catalog
- Links to subscription databases
- Links to suggested Web sites for research
- Book lists, booktalks, book suggestions, etc.

Keep It Current

Like other Web sites, yours must maintain currency in order to be useful. Library news, special events, and a library calendar are of no use if they are from six months ago. Links to good Web sites for research are useless if you don't check them periodically to make sure they are still working. Leaving the same ten book suggestions up all year makes that part of your site pointless. Be sure to keep the information on your site up to date. Items like "Quote of the Day" or "Today's Headlines" are useful and catchy, but remove them if you cannot devote the time to changing them every day (RSS feeds can be used to keep that type of information updated). A time saver for you might be to assign your aide, a volunteer, or student helpers to check certain parts of the site each week for needed updates.

Libraries in the Cyber World (Web 2.0)

There are many other ways and places to meet library users where they are. Whole books could be devoted to a discussion of online tools (sometimes called Web 2.0 tools) that users may access and use every day. People use these tools to network professionally and personally, find information, learn new skills or hobbies, advertise, and more. Librarians of today have the added challenge of learning about these tools and how to use them so that they can be incorporated into the menu of services offered to library users. After all, your teachers are using many of these Web 2.0 tools in their classrooms, so you will need to become familiar with them, also.

As a new school librarian, you will want to explore these tools and experiment with several to see if they improve service and are useful to your school community. You should find out school policy regarding use of some of these tools/sites; for example, school administration may require some way to filter inappropriate language/photos. Some of the Web 2.0 tools and Internet sites using these tools are the following:

- Blogs: A blog (Web log) is an online diary, a daily or weekly log, similar to writing in an open diary where multiple people can write their thoughts and comments. Basically, it's a "free-form" method of communication. Consider starting a blog on your school library Web site to share your thoughts and ideas with your school community and to get feedback and opinions from faculty and students.

- Chat: Several companies, like Yahoo, MSN, etc., offer free chat services that allow people to create a login and then communicate in real time to others by typing into a chat window. Depending on the host service, users can trade pictures, share Web links, initiate audio or video chat, and more. Libraries can use this tool to offer online reference assistance, similar to over-the-phone reference help.

- MySpace, Facebook, and Twitter: These are social networking sites that allow people to create a free account, post pictures, blog, add friends, etc. Libraries can use this tool to create an account that

---

SAMPLE ONLINE NETWORKING SITES

Library Blogs

Bullard Library
http://bullardlibrary.edublogs.org/

Ensworth Libraries
http://ensworth-libraries.blogspot.com/

LibraryStuff: A Weblog by Steven Cohen
http://www.librarystuff.net/

Library Web Chic
http://www.librarywebchic.net/wordpress/

Not So Distant Future
http://futura.edublogs.org/

Steven's Spotlight: Library Media Center 2.0
http://blogs.glnd.k12.va.us/teachers/astevens/

Sintoblog: A blog on library and information management
http://sintoblog.blogspot.com/

Tame the Web: Libraries, Technology and People
http://tametheweb.com/

Voices from the Inglenook (Cold Spring School Library)
http://csslibraryblog.blogspot.com/

You Tube pages

Carleton middle school library-stop motion
http://www.youtube.com/watch?v=0DqnAmjlSdg&
    feature=related

Elementary School Librarian
http://www.youtube.com/watch?v=xWGJw6O8_k8&
    feature=related

Ilovelibraries.org: Libraries on YouTube
http://www.ilovelibraries.org/loveyourlibrary/
    ILoveLibrariesonYouTube.cfm

School Library Media Specialist: my library, my life
http://www.youtube.com/watch?v=h8dSUSxpyeE&
    feature=related

School Library Media Centers Rock!
http://www.youtube.com/watch?v=faP3-M0ypaw&
    feature=related

Web and L.I.Brary
http://www.youtube.com/watch?v=JrFTD_KSGm8

MySpace Pages

Books for Boys by Michael Sullivan: Author, Reading Specialist, Storyteller
http://blogs.myspace.com/talestoldtall

Brooklyn College Library
http://www.myspace.com/brooklyncollegelibrary

Bryant University Library
http://www.myspace.com/bryantuniversitylibrary

Librarian in Black by Sarah Houghton-Jan
http://www.myspace.com/sarahhoughton

PCL and the UT Libraries
http://www.myspace.com/utlibraries

THE LIBRARY FAIRY!
http://profile.myspace.com/index.cfm?fuseaction=user
    .viewProfile&friendID=234586119

Wikis

ATN Reading Lists
http://atn-reading-lists.wikispaces.com/

users can request to be "friends" of and then post events, blog booktalks, share good Web sites, etc.

- Delicious: This is a social bookmarking site that allows people to create a free account and keep Web site bookmarks stored online. Members can then access their lists of favorites from any computer connected to the Internet. An added feature is that members can share their bookmarks with others by allowing them to view the lists. Libraries can use this tool by creating lists of bookmarks to author Web sites, educational games, information sites related to a school project theme, etc.

- YouTube: This is a video publishing site that allows people to create an account and then upload videos to share with others; browsing and viewing posted videos does not require membership. Libraries can use this tool to offer instructional videos on effective online research, note taking, library orientation, equipment training, etc.

- Second Life: A virtual world that allows people to create a free account and then create an online character (an avatar) for themselves that is used to explore the virtual world and interact with other members. Users can talk to one another, visit one another's homes, purchase and sell items, and more. Some libraries have created virtual libraries within Second Life that users can visit to do research, read electronic books, receive assistance from a virtual librarian, etc.

Connecting Library Users to Resources

You have great books waiting to be read and wonderful online resources waiting to be researched. Some of your students and teachers know how to get to them, but some do not. The resources are wasted if they are not used—and that's where you come in.

Reference Interview

The reference interview is a way to connect library users to the resources they want or need. It sounds stuffy and formal, but it is basically a conversation you have with a library user to help him or her figure out what he or she is looking for and then either find it or help the user to find the information. The reference interview is especially useful with students who don't frequent the library often, are not avid readers, or lack the information-seeking skills required to locate a reference book or online resource.

The following are the four basic steps to the reference interview:

- Receiving the request
- Evaluating and organizing how to address the request
- Locating the best information to answer the question
- Connecting the library user with the information needed to answer his or her question

It's sometimes hard to separate each step, as the whole process should flow together smoothly. While you may think that students will require the most help, remember that the rest of your school community, including teachers and administrators, often will need help in determining their question and locating relevant information.

Atmosphere (Receiving the Request)

Having the right atmosphere is the key to the reference interview. If you are a librarian who frowns at children, constantly shushes them, and has a "Do

Not Disturb" sign on your desk, you will probably not get the opportunity to conduct a reference interview. Most likely, you are not that librarian. Because you welcome students and teachers, greet them with a smile, and are always ready to offer help, your library users feel comfortable enough to ask you for assistance in locating resources in your library. Encourage students to seek you out by placing signs in the library directing them to you for help, and mingle with library users and ask, "Is there anything I can help you with today?" Even if they do not come to you with a question, you can often see when someone is in need of help; don't hesitate to offer your help.

Determining Need (Evaluating the Request and Locating Information)

The most important step in the reference interview process is to determine the library user's need. This may seem simple, like asking, "What is it you are looking for today?" This is actually only the beginning phase of determining need. Often, users' actual needs are different from the ones they voice. It is up to you to discover their true needs by repeating, rephrasing, and asking questions to expand on or narrow the request. Listen in on this reference interview between a librarian (L) and elementary student (S):

L: Can I help you find something today?

S: Yes, Mrs. Booker. I want a book about snakes.

L: Snakes. Okay. Let's go to the animal section of the library—that's in the five-hundreds. Are you looking for books about a specific type of snake, like a cobra or python?

S: No. Just about snakes. But not big ones.

L: Are you doing a research project about snakes?

S: No. I want a book for home. I'm getting a pet snake today.

L: Oh. So do you need a book about different types of snakes so you can choose the one you want?

S: No. My dad already bought one. He's picking it up on the way home from work today.

L: What kind of information did you want to read about snakes?

S: What they live in and eat and stuff like that.

L: Have you ever had a pet snake before?

S: No . . . and I don't know what to do with it.

L: I think you're probably looking for a book that tells how to take care of a snake. It would tell you how to make a good home for it and feed it.

S: Yes, that's what I need.

L: Great. I know exactly which books you want. Let's go to the six-hundreds and look in the pet section for a book about pet snakes or reptiles.

In this case, the student knew what she needed but did not phrase it exactly right in the beginning. Now listen in on a reference interview between a librarian (L) and a high school student (S) in which the student does not actually know what he needs:

S: Mr. Booker, I need help!

L: I'd be glad to help. What are you looking for?

S: I need information about Edgar Allen Poe for an assignment.

L: Do you have a copy of the assignment sheet with you?

S: No. I lost it. Mr. Smith wants us to write an essay about Poe.

L: Alright. What type of information do you need in the essay?

S: About his life and stuff.

L: We have several biographies about Poe. Is that all you need?

S: I think so.

L: Can you tell me about the assignment?

S: We have to write about how Poe's life shaped his writing.

L: Oh. So biographies will help us know about events in his life. What else would we need to know in order to do the comparison?

S: About his writings.

L: So we probably need to get a book about his life and a collection of his writings. Does Mr. Smith want you to use books or computer resources?

S: He doesn't care.

L: Great. Let's go get the biography and the Poe collection, and then I'll show you some databases and Web sites you might use.

Connecting the User with the Resource

In the previous two scenarios, the school librarian has determined the student's information need and decided on some resources that will answer the question. As indicated, the final step is to connect the user with the resources. Part of this process is being sure that the resources do, in fact, answer the question at hand.

After bringing the library user and resource together, continue the interview with follow-up. Make sure you've given the student what he or she was looking for and that it will be a useful resource. Show some other resources (print and electronic) that might further help with the information need. Let the student know he or she should come back if this resource ends up not being useful so that you can help locate exactly what is really needed.

Interviews and Student Interests

Similar to a reference interview for research topics, sometimes you will need to help a student just find a book to read. Students who are not avid readers and are not familiar with authors or books in your collection may brave the library doors and come searching for leisure reading for the weekend, or their mean teacher might make them check out a book for class reading. This is an opportunity to connect students to the right books that might turn them on to reading and get them to visit and check out books on a regular basis. The good news is that they have come to you as a blank slate.

The bad news is that they have come to you as a blank slate. They have no idea what books or types of books they would like, and the answer to most of your questions will be, "I don't know...I never read." The trick is to tap into their areas of interest without having them think about books. If you can discover what they like, you can find them a book to read. Even though they may not be big fans of books, they will thumb through or even read books that contain topics of interest to them. Figure 15-1 offers some questions you might use to help determine student interests.

Displays (Anticipating User Needs)

After you determine topics of research and areas of interest of your school community, become a proactive librarian. Rather than waiting for individual students to ask you for help finding these books, create displays of books you know they want or need. If the science classes are working on recycling projects, display the books you have about recycling on a table covered with grocery bags and intersperse empty and cleaned cans and bottles. If you have noticed more students checking out books about current singers, pull some of the books and put them on a display stand with old CDs attached all around it. If the school started a knitting club, pull those books and put them in a display window with skeins of yarn and a knitting needle poked into a sweater. Connecting library users with resources is all about determining and fulfilling users' needs; if you can determine some of those needs ahead of time, you can get those resources into students' hands faster by bringing them out and putting them within easy reach.

Figure 15-1. Student Interest Inventory Questions

What is the title of a book you remember reading and enjoying?	What are two things you dislike?
What do you watch on television?	What are two things you like very much?
Name some of your favorite movies.	Who is someone you admire?
Do you have any hobbies? What do you do in your free time?	If you could go on a vacation anywhere, where would you go?
What sports do you enjoy watching or playing (even if just for fun)?	If a genie granted you three wishes, what would you wish for?
What job(s) will you have in the future if you could choose any?	If you wrote a book, what would it be about?

Library Media Specialist as Teacher and Instructional Specialist

Repeat this line: "I am much more than the keeper of books in my school."

You will soon discover that school librarians wear several different hats. Sometimes you will rapidly change from one hat to another in a blur, and often you will wear a few at the same time (trying to balance them so they don't all fall off). The good news is that you are more than capable of fulfilling all of the roles.

One of your most important roles in the building will be that of teacher and instructional specialist. You most likely will have some classroom experience under your belt, and it will definitely come in handy to you as the school's librarian. Although you don't have a traditional classroom and a regular set of students to call your own, you do have an instructional area in the building (probably one of the largest), and all of the students in the building are your students. They will look to you for guidance and instruction, and teachers will look to you for support and ideas. Your building administrators will hopefully see you as a specialist who can enhance classroom instruction, and your position and schedule should afford you the opportunity to do just that. You might even be a member of your school's instructional leadership team that makes decisions about how to help teachers and students be more successful.

This role is very rewarding as it allows you to impact the entire school and make a difference in what students are learning and how teachers are engaging them in that learning.

Learning the School's Curriculum

An interesting aspect of being an instructional librarian is that, unlike teachers who teach one or a few grade levels or content areas, you must be slightly familiar with all subjects that are being taught in your school. Before you panic, this is not to say that you must know every aspect of every course in your school; it simply means that you must have an overview of what students are learning. Knowing the curriculum will help you make decisions about collection development, but it will also make you a valuable resource to all teachers in your building. Your school may have grade level or content specialists that oversee and work with teachers in their particular area; your area of specialty is, well, everything. Your information skills must allow you to locate materials to support all subjects being taught in your school.

Learn about the Curriculum

Learning about what each teacher is teaching will come with time, and it will change constantly as the faculty and curriculum change. You will get to know gradually your teachers and the textbooks and will become fairly knowledgeable about the school's curriculum. For now, however, try to get a general idea of the topics or themes that are being covered in your building as the school year begins. This will allow you to proactively help and support the faculty from the beginning rather than waiting for them to seek you out.

A good place to start is by getting copies of the curriculum. A school in a large district might follow a curriculum written at the district level and used at all campuses in that district. Small districts and private schools may write their own curriculum within the building. You should be able to get a copy of the curriculum either online, at your district or school office, or from specialists or department chairs within the school. Although some curricular guides can be very detailed, even spelling out what is taught on a particular day or week, browsing them will give you an idea of types of content being taught.

You will end up with many curriculum guides representing different content areas or grade levels. When you have a little spare time (ha-ha), you might want to condense the information into an easier-to-use format like the one shown in Figure 16-1. Personalize this form based on your school's grading schedule, grade levels or content areas, etc. To start with, you might focus on finding out just the topics being covered during the first grading period and then fill in the rest gradually; just don't forget to finish completing the form. Writing down the basic information in one place creates a simple sheet that you can refer to when making book choices or designing activities, lessons, events, displays, etc. Imagine how valuable you would be to your

Figure 16-1 School Curriculum Overview

	1st nine weeks: topics	2nd nine weeks: topics	3rd nine weeks: topics	4th nine weeks: topics
7th English	EX: Narrative writing, "self" in literature, grammar review			
8th English				
7th Math	EX: Problem-solving process, integers, decimals, patterns			
8th Math				
7th Science				
8th Science	EX: Lab safety, scientific inquiry, matter			
7th Social Studies				
8th Social Studies				
Health				
Art	EX: Profiles, figure drawing, texture and value			
Theater				
Music				
Speech				

faculty if you knew that second grade would begin a unit on insects in two weeks and you set up a bulletin board with pictures and diagrams of different insects, put the insect books on a display table, scheduled a "bug expert" from the local nature sanctuary to visit the school, and made a bookmark listing URLs of high-quality, educational, and fun Web sites about insects.

Attend Meetings

Another way to stay current on what is being taught is to attend planning meetings with your school's teachers, chairs, and specialists. Although it would probably be impossible to attend every planning meeting, make a point to attend several each month. Visit with different grade levels or content teams. Actively listen during the meetings, take notes, and be prepared to offer suggestions or assistance when appropriate. Make the most of this time you spend at meetings; it allows you to show interest, make or strengthen relationships with the faculty, and become aware of ways to support your teachers. In addition to general planning meetings, ask to participate in the curriculum development process in your school district. Your knowledge of educational resources can be invaluable to the curriculum development team in your school and will show administration that you are both interested and committed to the educational role of your job as school library media specialist.

Visit Classrooms

A great way to know what is going on is to occasionally leave your library and "roam the streets," so to speak. Walk down a hall and see what teachers and students are doing. Visit a classroom or two (you might need to schedule this in advance) and mingle. Witnessing students exploring and discovering and listening to teachers guiding them might just spark a few good ideas you can bring back to your library or next planning meeting. You might even find yourself rushing back to Ms. Bailey's classroom to say, "As I sat in here earlier and participated with your students, I remembered a book I recently ordered that goes wonderfully with what you're teaching. I just had to bring it to you so you could see it!"

Collaborating with Teachers

Now that you've looked around and figured out what people are teaching and learning in your building (librarians are the best detectives), it is time to put this knowledge to good use. Your teachers and their students could benefit from your input. You have resources at your disposal that can enhance instruction, including books, audiovisuals, databases, and the Internet. You also have ideas for lessons and activities that could make learning fun and effective. Collaboration with teachers makes you a vital part of your school. Your school could keep track of books in a much less expensive way than having you on the payroll, so you must show that you can do much more for the students and staff. Since teaching is the number one priority at your school, it's important for you to become a crucial member of the team.

Reeling Them In

The most important thing to remember is that you must actively seek collaboration opportunities. If you wait for teachers to come to you when they need help, you might be waiting for a very long time. Teachers are overwhelmed with responsibilities and mandates, and the spare moments they have to seek out help will most likely not be spent with you unless you have shown yourself to be an instructional asset. The traditional, stereotypical view of a librarian is one of a stern bookworm who prefers isolation and quiet. Since most teacher preparation courses do not include much (or any) instruction on the role and value of a school librarian, it will be up to you to break this stereotype and show teachers everything you can do for them. Once teachers know what you have to offer in terms of instructional collaboration, they will be knocking down doors to get to you; before this can happen, though, you must make the first move.

Here are a few ways to seek out collaboration opportunities:

- Attend planning meetings and participate. Consider offering the library as a meeting place for planning meetings and offer refreshments—once you have them cornered and bribed with food, they are all yours.

- Keep your eyes and ears open. "Snoop" in the halls, listening for opportunities to provide resources or lesson/activity planning ideas.

- Ask a content specialist, department chair, or administrator to pair you with a teacher who needs support or would enjoy working with you to do some lesson planning and teaching.

- Choose a guinea pig in the faculty (friends and new teachers work well for this) and tell him or her you'd love to sit for a few minutes to hear what he or she will be teaching soon so you can help find materials or plan a fun lesson.

- Advertise on the school's Web site, by e-mail, school newspaper, etc., offering your collaboration services.

- Ask to give a two-minute presentation at the next faculty meeting so you can entice teachers to collaborate with you on an upcoming lesson.

The Collaboration Meeting

Once you have convinced a teacher to let you work with him or her, set up a time to sit down and talk. Sometimes you will have to take the opportunity to hold a collaboration meeting with a teacher at the copy machine or bathroom sink, but having a real meeting with time to go over details and ideas is a better approach. It would benefit you to find out the general topic for the lesson (like "photosynthesis" or "Julius Caesar") before the meeting so that you can come to the table with a few ideas and materials. Figure 17-1 presents a sample form that you could use to gather information about the teacher's needs in advance of your initial meeting.

Some teachers will enthusiastically welcome any and all input you have and will gladly let you mastermind a lesson for them; some are territorial and might only be humoring you to see if you have anything to offer. It is important to start the meeting by listening. Hear what content the teacher wants to teach and find out any initial thoughts and ideas he or she may have. Build on these ideas by adding your knowledge of the content, provide access to materials that can support the lesson, and work with the teacher to develop an engaging lesson or activity to reach his or her goal.

It may benefit you to have a collaboration note-taking form handy to use during these types of meetings (see Figure 17-2). The form will help you get all of the information down in one place and can remind you and the teacher of things to consider. Keep copies of completed forms to serve as a record of the collaboration for ideas, future meetings, or future lesson planning needs, or if your supervisor wants to know how you are supporting instruction in the school. Warning: These types of forms can appear intimidating, so use them with care and don't scare away a potential collaborating teacher by saying, "Wait...I need to get the official form so I can record what we're saying." If teachers appear more comfortable in a less-formal setting without immediate note taking or with notes jotted on a scrap sheet of paper, do that instead.

Figure 17-1. Teacher/Librarian Research Collaboration Form

* Please plan to meet with the librarian at least once prior to starting this project. *

Teacher: _____

Research topic: _____

Dates for research in library: _____

Period: 1st ☐ 2nd ☐ 3rd ☐ 4th ☐ 5th ☐ 6th ☐ 7th ☐ 8th ☐

What is your goal for the students?

What preparations need to be done with your class prior to beginning this project?

Preparation/Skill	By Teacher	By Librarian

How will students work?   individually _____   pairs _____   groups of _____

What is(are) the possible end product(s)?

Class will use the following resources:

	Encyclopedias/Reference books
	Non-fiction books
	Electronic databases
	Internet
	Printer
	Copier
	Other

Figure 17-2. Collaboration Meeting Notes

Date: _____

Teacher's name: _____

Grade level/content area: _____

Estimated dates for lesson/unit/project: _____

Topic: _____

What do you want students to learn by the end?

_____

_____

How will students obtain the information? (*check all that apply*)

_____ individual research

_____ reading (books, textbooks, magazines, etc.)

_____ computer use (databases, Web sites, etc.)

_____ information provided to them in print

_____ information provided to them verbally

Desired end product: (*check all that apply*)

_____ written document   _____ slideshow

_____ graphics/illustrations   _____ movie

_____ text plus graphics (specify below)   _____ Web page

_____ performance (specify below)   _____ other (specify below)

Materials needed (projector, art supplies, digital camera, Web sites, etc.):

_____

_____

Does library time or librarian time need to be scheduled?   ___ Yes   ___ No

Things we need to plan/prepare (vocabulary sheet, online form, map, etc.):

_____

_____

_____

Should we create a sample for students to see before/as they work?   ___ Yes   ___ No

Follow-up meeting date and time: _____

Your Part of the Preparation Work

After the meeting, it is time to begin working on your part of the lesson or activity. During the meeting, the teacher and you should have agreed on the breakdown of the workload for this lesson. Encourage the teacher to do what he or she is best at—writing up the official lesson plan, designing how the lesson will be implemented, making decisions about grading, dividing students into functional groups, etc. You have individual skills and talents, and there are also tasks you are good at because you are the librarian. Your part of the work might include the following:

- Scheduling library time, if needed
- Finding informational resources for the content, such as books, magazine articles, Web sites, etc.
- Acquiring support materials, such as videos, photos, audio recordings, etc.
- Helping create materials needed for the lesson, like worksheets, posters, slideshows, podcasts, a movie, etc.
- Creating online content, like accessible lists of Web sites or an online version of the lesson with accompanying materials linked

To Teach . . . or Not to Teach?

It might be appropriate for you to teach a specific part of the lesson (like how to use the databases to find information for research) or even for you to co-teach during the entire duration of the lesson. There are benefits to offering your services as a teacher. It allows you to keep your teacher-brain from becoming rusty. It also reminds the faculty and administration that you are a member of the instructional team in the school. It helps strengthen your relationship with students. It allows you to be a big part of the lesson you helped design and lets you see how successful (or not) it was when actually implemented.

The disadvantage of teaching lessons is that it takes time away from being the librarian. Granted, the time is well-spent doing something very important and something you want to be doing as a school librarian. However, you must be careful to manage your time so that you are not spending so much time teaching that you cannot successfully manage the library. Also, be sure you are not taken advantage of and constantly put into a position of teaching in place of the teacher. Nothing is more frustrating than to plan collaboratively, offer to co-teach the lesson, and then watch the classroom teacher walk out of the room just as you begin teaching.

Advertising . . . Again

After a few successful collaborative efforts, spread the word! Once you have convinced some teachers of your usefulness, others are sure to follow. Ask the teachers you worked with to do some word-of-mouth advertising to let other teachers know what you can do for them. Have someone take pictures of you and the teacher working with students during the lesson and post them. Write up your experiences in your newsletter, post it on your library's Web page, or make a short presentation at a faculty meeting. Show teachers how excited you are about collaborating with them to make their jobs easier and their students even more successful.

Providing Research Instruction

One subject that teachers will willingly collaborate with you on, and probably come to you desperately seeking assistance with, is research. You are in a unique position in that you have within arm's length the bulk of the research resources in your building. Being the overseer of these resources allows you the opportunity to play a positive and active role in the instruction and guidance of research in your school; take advantage of it because it is one of the most powerful instructional opportunities you have.

"Information literacy" is a buzz word in libraries and in education, and it is even becoming a hot topic in the corporate world as well. As technology continues to improve daily and our society continues to be inundated with information at dizzying speeds, it is crucial that people be able to identify their information needs, know where to find information, and be able to synthesize it to make it meaningful to them. This is where research instruction comes in. Your students must learn now how to locate and manage all of the information around them so that they can become successful and productive adults. Most schools include research instruction somewhere in the curriculum, but often teachers are left to figure out how to go about it on their own. This is a perfect time for you as librarian to step in and offer your help.

Planning Research Lessons

The best way to ensure the quality of research instruction in your school is to be a part of the planning process. As mentioned in earlier chapters, meeting with grade level and content chairs and teachers is vital; research instruction is definitely a team effort. The curriculum may specify a time line and topics for research, but it most likely will not. In your interactions with teachers in your building, try to determine when the best times of the year will be for you to devote time and energy to high-quality research instruction. For example, the weeks before state tests and the last weeks of school are usually *not* good times to schedule research. Look at the topics being taught and select several that lend themselves to research lessons or projects.

Work with your teachers to create research activities that are a good fit for them, their curriculum, and their students. Here are some tips:

- Decide the appropriate level of complexity for the activity. Is it more appropriate as a short research mini-lesson—like an information hunt—or as a lengthy project with notes, paper, citations, etc.?

- Allow students some choices of topic—their choice of any civil rights personality rather than all students researching Dr. Martin Luther King, Jr., for example.

- Choose an overarching topic that offers a wide scope of subtopics for research. For example, "female athletes" would work better than "female golfers."

- Allow students to synthesize and then be creative rather than regurgitate information. It is more fun and a better learning experience when students can design and describe their own new planet in our solar system rather than copying down information about one of the eight planets in existence.

- Be sure you have (or can obtain) information resources that students will need to complete their assignment.

- Make a realistic time line for the research activity that allows a little extra time if needed so that students are not frustrated by the experience of an impossible research task.

- Decide what research skills will need to be reviewed or taught, decide who will teach them, and plan on being available to assist students during the research process.

Individual Learning Styles

Everyone learns in different ways, and students are no different. In order to provide better research instruction to students, and also to enhance your role as a collaborator with teachers (see Chapter 17), you need to understand your students' information needs, knowledge level, interests, and preferred learning styles.

Some of the ways to determine student learning style are to give a pretest, observe students in the media center, consult with their teachers, or distribute a survey or inventory to assess student learning styles. As librarian, you should develop a collection of materials that will accommodate different learning styles; be sure that your teachers know what is available. In addition, you will need to have the tools available to assess student learning styles. Many learning style inventories are available for use in the library media center, from simple observation and paper/pencil tests to more sophisticated tests with computerized scoring. One of the best assessment tools is the Learning Style Type Indicator, developed by John W. Pelley at the Texas Tech University. This simple-to-administer test is based on the Myers-Briggs Type Indicator for personality types and provides statistically valid results. The introduction/background information about the test can be found at www.ttuhsc.edu/SOM/Success/page_LSTI/LSTIIntro.htm; it's helpful to read this background before administering the test. The test itself is located at www.ttuhsc.edu/ SOM/Success/page_LSTI/LSTI.htm. The student can go to the Web site and respond to the questions that best describe his or her comfort level of working. At the end, the student receives a code for his or her learning style and can click a link to read about the characteristics of that learning type.

Instruction: Taking Notes

One of the research skills students struggle with most is taking notes. With the widespread availability and use of the Internet, students know how to find information fairly quickly. When it comes to researching the information and submitting it to a teacher, however, many students believe a two-minute search, find, copy, paste, and print is the complete process. Teachers should be instructing students on proper note taking so as to foster information synthesis and avoid plagiarism. As the school librarian, you need to be an expert in the skill of taking notes because it is one that often becomes an issue in the library. Students must be shown how to read information, process it mentally, and then jot down only minimal words or phrases that represent the main ideas of the information they need to complete the assignment. Find out if your school or district has adopted a research model such as Big 6 or I-Search (see the note at the end of this chapter for more information on Big 6 and I-Search) so that you can review note-taking formats that go with that model. You might also want to look at note-taking ideas such as Cornell Notes and Trash-N-Treasure. Several models and techniques are already in use that can be adopted or modified, or feel free to create your own technique if it works for your student population and teachers' needs.

In 2007, the American Association of School Librarians adopted *Standards for the 21st-Century Learner* (American Association of School Librarians, 2007), which details 29 discrete skills that students should be able to perform to complete a research project (see Figure 18-1). You should familiarize yourself with these skills and be able to teach them to the students (see Figure 18-2). More detailed information about these skills is available at www.ala.org/aasl/standards.

Instruction: Resource Use

Students will also need guidance or instruction on using the resources that are available for finding information in the library and on the Internet. At the elementary level, you will need to teach skills such as finding books in the catalog, using call numbers, navigating on prescreened Web sites, etc. At the secondary level, you will need to review some of those more basic skills as well as teach Boolean search logic, database navigation, etc. Although students spend hours every day doing things on their computers that you wish you knew how to do, remember that they often feel lost and intimidated in your library. You and the teacher might decide that a formal lesson is needed before research begins—for example, teaching a class how to use a specific database that they will need to use for a project. Alternately, you

Figure 18-1. Summary of Information Literacy Skills from AASL's *Standards for the 21st-Century Learner*

Standard	Summary of Skills
Inquire, think critically, and gain knowledge	• Follow an inquiry process • Develop and refine questions • Find, evaluate, and select appropriate sources • Evaluate information • Make sense of information gathered • Make use of technology tools • Collaborate with others to broaden and deepen understanding
Draw conclusions, make informed decisions, apply knowledge to new situations, and create new knowledge	• Apply critical thinking skills to construct new understandings, draw conclusions, and create new knowledge • Analyze and organize knowledge, making use of technology tools • Collaborate with others to exchange ideas
Share knowledge and participate ethically and productively as members of our democratic society	• Use the writing process, visual literacy, and technology tools to express new understandings • Use information and technology ethically and responsibly
Pursue personal and aesthetic growth	• Read, view, and listen for pleasure and personal growth • Respond to creative expression of ideas • Seek information for personal learning • Organize personal knowledge • Use social networks to gather and share information • Use creative forms for expression

Source: Donham, Jean. 2008. *Enhancing Teaching and Learning: A Leadership Guide for School Library Media Specialists* (p. 239), 2nd Edition Revised. New York: Neal-Schuman.

might be doing mini-instruction as you walk around the library assisting students or offering one-on-one instruction when they come to you asking for help. Here are some topics you may need to teach or review in regard to the use of various resources:

- Books: searching in the catalog, reading call numbers and locating the book on the shelf, using the table of contents and index of a book, using headings and subheadings in the catalog

- Reference books: using an index volume, navigating by means of guide words, using "see" and "see also" references

- Databases: choosing the right database, selecting search terms and keywords, using Boolean logic, navigating the search screen, using "find" or "locate" functions to pinpoint information, using additional links to get more information, recognizing formats (e.g., journal article, newspaper, etc.)

- Web sites: Boolean search logic, choosing good sites (reliable, accurate, and current), determining author or creator for establishing authority or bias, finding or filtering to get "just what I need," cross-checking information for verification

Figure 18-2. Skills for the 21st-Century Learner

* Today's students must learn how to use technology, clearly communicate ideas, and interact sensitively with others.

* Information Literacy is no longer just "using reference resources to find information." Learners must also now be competent in multiple literacies, including digital, visual, textual, and technological.

21st-Century Learners use skills, resources, and tools to:

1. inquire, think critically, and gain knowledge;
2. draw conclusions, make informed decisions, apply knowledge to new situations, and create new knowledge;
3. share knowledge and participate ethically and productively as members of our democratic society;
4. pursue personal and aesthetic growth.

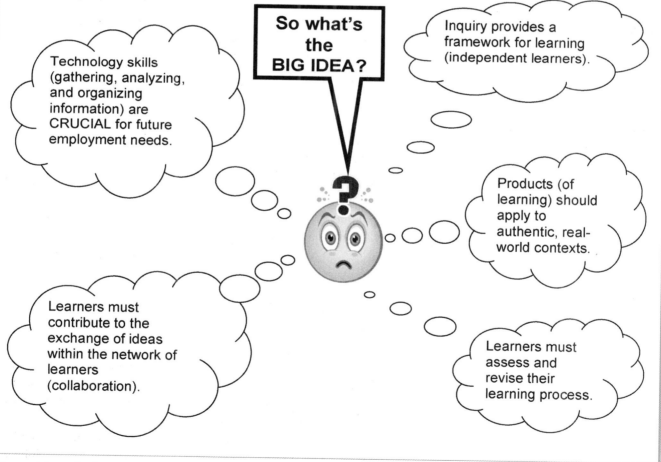

So what's the BIG IDEA?

Technology skills (gathering, analyzing, and organizing information) are CRUCIAL for future employment needs.

Inquiry provides a framework for learning (independent learners).

Products (of learning) should apply to authentic, real-world contexts.

Learners must contribute to the exchange of ideas within the network of learners (collaboration).

Learners must assess and revise their learning process.

Source: Information from American Association of School Librarians. 2007. *Standards for the 21st-Century Learner.* Chicago: American Library Association.

Instruction: Citing References and Plagiarism

While teaching students how to research and guiding them about resource use, you might want to take the opportunity to do some instruction on intellectual property and plagiarism. Because of the vast amount of information available to them publicly via the Internet, students often think they can simply find and take what they need. It is important that you teach them that they may reference information they find as long as they give credit to the source. Like taking money from someone's purse, taking information is stealing, and it is a crime. Talk to students briefly about the importance of protecting and respecting another person's work and property by giving credit when borrowing information. Show them where to get the information for the citation and how to format it depending on the style you or their teacher prefers: MLA (Modern Language Association) or APA (American Psychological Association), etc. You might want to do a two-minute presentation before a class begins a research project so that you won't need to do as much one-on-one instruction later. Teachers are usually more than happy to give you the floor for this important mini-lesson, especially if you prepare all the visuals and handouts yourself. Be prepared for a situation in which the teacher has not considered requiring citations or does not know exactly how to do citations himself or herself; in these cases it will be up to you to do all of the instruction (to both students and teacher) and possibly assist the teacher in outlining citation requirements for the project and helping the teacher grade that portion. Some Web sites that might help you are the following:

Citation Machine
http://citationmachine.net/

Purdue Online Writing Lab
http://owl.english.purdue.edu/owl/

Long Island University library citation styles
www.liu.edu/cwis/cwp/library/workshop/citation.htm

Organization: The Research Folder

Consider creating an organizational tool that will help make the research process a little less formidable for you, the teachers, and the students. One such tool is a research folder (see Figures 18-3 and 18-4). The premise is that the folder is a place for students to store paperwork associated with the activity or project. It provides a place to take notes and keep all of the reference details about the project together in one location. Buy some inexpensive folders and find out if you can get someone (either your district's print shop or a commercial printing service) to print helpful information on both the outside and inside of the folder; this makes it more difficult for students to lose sheets, and you reduce paper usage and waste. You can include sheets of printouts and have them stapled into the folder. What you

Figure 18-3. Front of a Research Folder

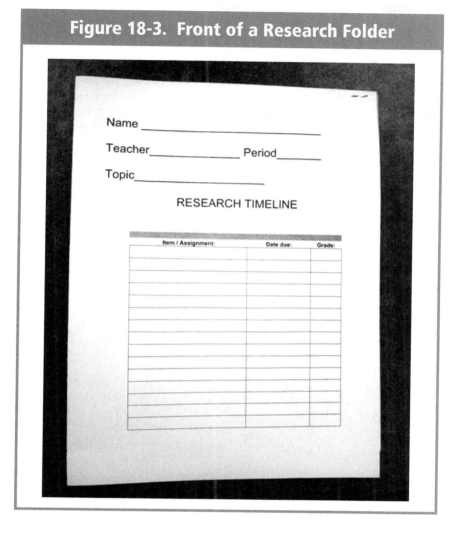

include in the folder depends on the grade levels you work with and teacher needs. Some things you might include on or in the folder are the following:

- A place for identification information—student name, date, subject, teacher, class period, etc.
- A place to list the topic for research
- A time line students can use for due dates or to track progress
- A sheet of citation help and examples
- Space for listing sources used
- Spaces or boxes for brainstorming, graphic organizer, etc.
- Note-taking sheet(s)
- Space for pasting or drawing diagrams, pictures, etc.
- Listing of databases or Web sites, access passwords, hints for using electronic resources, etc.
- A general research rubric or space for a teacher-created one; see Figure 18-5 for a general research rubric that students can use for

Figure 18-4. Inside of a Research Folder

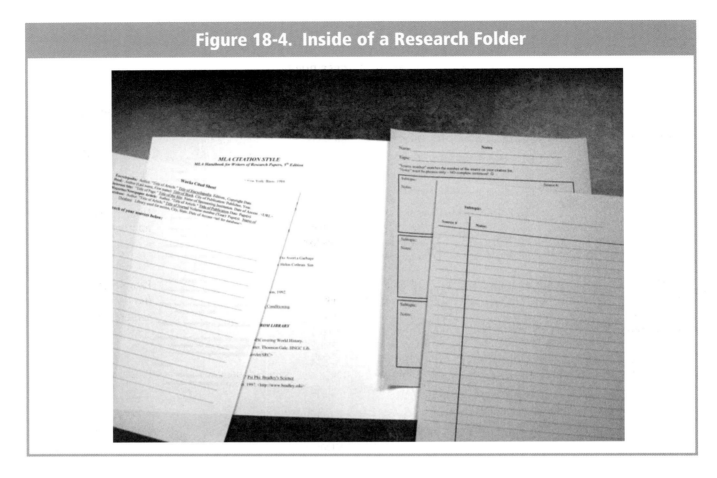

self-evaluation during the process and teachers can use to grade the final project (this can be printed on the back of the research folder)

Be sure to personalize the folder to your school's needs. Make it a useful tool that you believe in and want to use with your faculty and staff. Once you create it, advertise it. Present the research folder at team meetings or faculty meetings and get your department chairs or specialists on board. Show it to students and offer it to anyone who appears to be working on research in your library. When a teacher collaborates with you and sets up library time, ask him or her how many research folders he or she will need for class. Instruct students on how to use them effectively to make research easier and more organized. Be ready to order more; once teachers and students get their hands on them, they will go like hotcakes!

For More Information on Research Skills

For more information on the Big 6 method of research, consult this resource:

> Eisenberg, Michael B. 1990. *Information Problem Solving: The Big6 Skills Approach to Library and Information Skills Instruction*. New York: Ablex.

Be sure to see "Guided Inquiry" at: http://cissl.scils.rutgers.edu/guided_inquiry/introduction.html

Kuhlthau, Carol. 2007. *Guided Inquiry: Learning in the 21st Century*. Santa Barbara, CA: Libraries Unlimited.

Figure 18-5. General Research Rubric (Secondary Level)

RESEARCH PROCESS RUBRIC

	1 (0)	2 (70–79)	3 (80–89)	4 (90–100)
Question/Task	No research question/topic/thesis	Question/topic/thesis is vague and unclear	Question/topic/thesis is focused and clear	Question/topic/thesis is clear, focused, complete, and shows critical thinking
Locate resources	No resources used	Used few or inappropriate resources (e.g., search engines like Google)	Used some resources (perhaps not a variety) that were appropriate	Used multiple appropriate resources
Gather information (retelling/ note taking)	Completely plagiarized/cut and pasted/copied; no notes	Off-topic notes/research; bulk of notes using complete sentences rather than phrases	Not all notes are on topic; some complete sentences used in notes	Paraphrasing and notes (no complete sentences); all on topic
Citing sources	Sources not cited	Not enough or not cited properly	Cited properly with errors	Properly cited
Organize and present	Product or presentation does not meet criteria from project rubric	Product or presentation meets few criteria from project rubric; unclear and disorganized	Product or presentation meets most criteria from project rubric; clear and mostly organized	Product or presentation includes all criteria from project rubric; organized and clear
Evaluate	No self-evaluation done or apparent	Little evaluation or reflection done or apparent	Some evaluation or reflection done or apparent	In-depth evaluation or reflection done or apparent

overall grade: _____

For more information on the I-Search method, consult these resources:

Duncan, Donna, and Laura Lockhart. 2000. *I-Search, You Search, We All Learn to Research.* New York: Neal-Schuman.

Duncan, Donna, and Laura Lockhart. 2005. *I-Search for Success: A How-To-Do-It Manual for Linking the I-Search Process with Standards, Assessment, and Evidence-Based Practice.* New York: Neal-Schuman.

Joyce, Marilyn, and Julie Tallman. 1997. *Making the Writing and Research Connection with the I-Search Process.* New York: Neal-Schuman.

For more information on using the Internet for research, consult these resources:

Kroski, Ellysa. 2008. *Web 2.0 for Librarians and Information Professionals.* New York: Neal-Schuman.

Devine, Jane, and Francine Egger-Sider. 2009. *Going Beyond Google: The Invisible Web in Learning and Teaching.* New York: Neal-Schuman.

Reference

American Association of School Librarians. 2007. *Standards for the 21st-Century Learner*. Chicago: American Library Association. Available: http://www.ala.org/ala/mgrps/divs/aasl/aaslproftools/learningstandards/AASL_Learning_Standards_2007.pdf.

Offering Special Programming

Although your first impression might be that special programs do not really belong in the section about instruction, the programs you plan and provide do promote reading, learning, and discovery. Your flexible daily schedule, budget, connection to all grade levels and content and the resources at your disposal give you the ability to offer some special services and events that enhance classroom instruction and connect students to unique experiences. Your programming also promotes the library and attracts students who might otherwise not frequent your library.

Read-alouds

Read-aloud means much more than reading a book to a group of children in the library. It is an opportunity to share the joy of reading and expose children to high-quality and fun literature. It is a chance to interact with students in the place you love best, surrounded by wonderful books. It is a time to possibly get just one more child to fall in love with reading. It is a small chunk in your hectic day during which you can recharge your battery with the energy of children's laughter and smiling, eager faces.

Here are some tips for a successful read-aloud:

- Choose the book wisely. Connect it to something the class is learning: a holiday, a culture represented in your school, etc. Or pick a book that you know students will enjoy. Look for interesting language (verse, repetition, alliteration, etc.) and captivating pictures. Caldecott winners and runner-ups are a good place to start. Some may not be to your liking, so look through the list and review them.

- Read the book and become familiar with it before the read-aloud. It may contain some questionable words or situations that make you rethink the choice. Even if the book is just what you wanted, there may be tricky language—tongue twisters or foreign words, for example—that you don't want to be surprised by during the read-aloud.

- Get vocally creative. Use inflection, even if you must exaggerate, to set the tone and make the story more interesting. If the mood strikes you, use different voices for dramatic effect and to make the characters come alive. Feel free to break into song when appropriate.

- Consider some movement or dramatization. You might have students repeat some hand or body movements that go with the story (like the gestures that go with "The Wheels on the Bus"). You could also have students participate in acting out parts of the story—for example, having five students be the five little monkeys as you read the story. Getting audience participation makes the story even better.

- Most of the students attending will want to check out the book that you just read aloud to them. Have a list or display ready of other books that are comparable: "If you liked ____, check out ____". This is a great way to take advantage of students' excitement and introduce them to other great literature.

- Take the opportunity to collaborate. Meet with the teachers in advance and see if you can connect the read-aloud to what they are or will be teaching. The book you choose could be an introductory piece to new content that the class will be working on soon. You might even be able to create a fun sheet or activity the teacher can utilize in the classroom after the read-aloud.

- For very young children, you may want to start with a song or game that gets them excited about the story, but you'll want to be sure they are settled down enough to hear it. Have some preestablished rules and hand signals for redirection during the read-aloud. You might end with a song or game that relates to the story, reinforces the theme or subject matter, and gives them a fun way to end the session and exit the library.

Storytelling

Storytelling is an entirely different being. It is a skill and an art form. Throughout history, storytellers have been a vital part of society; they kept mental records of the people's history before the printed word was accessible, and they entertained peasants and royalty alike with their tales. The story that they told was never exactly the same twice, and often the embellishments in the story depended on who was seated in the audience that day or who financially supported the storyteller. Even today people make a living by telling stories, and plenty of people love to listen to them. If your budget can allow it, you might consider hiring a professional storyteller. If you decide to try your hand at it, here are some tips:

- Choose a story you know or like. If you do not enjoy it or are not comfortable with it, your audience will know.

- Hold firm to only the major details of the story. A good storyteller adjusts the story slightly to suit the audience. You can change names, settings, phrases, etc. so that children will better connect to the story.

- Use vocal inflection and body language to help tell the story.
- Consider costume, background music or sound effects, props, etc.
- *Practice!* Use a mirror, a friend, your family, etc. Practicing will help you work out some of the flaws and make adjustments before the actual performance, and it will give you confidence.

Booktalks

Booktalks are a great way to promote literacy, "sell" books and your library, and keep you connected with students. They can be given to a large group in the library or in a classroom, to a single student in the hallway, over the public address or video delivery system, etc. Even a very short booktalk done as an intermission in a classroom can have a big effect on students. Living in such a media-rich society, take advantage of this opportunity to "do a commercial" and get children hooked on your product.

Here are some tips:

- Choose a book that students will be interested in; new books make good choices since you will be introducing them.
- Be familiar with the book; you can't sell it if you don't really know anything about it. Jot down notes on an index card that you can refer to during the talk.
- Bring the book with you to show to them, and make sure you mention the title and author more than once.
- Hook students and get them excited about the book. Don't just tell them what it is about. Share some juicy details or read an enticing excerpt.
- Tell enough about the story to get students interested, but don't give away all the best parts or the ending. Remember that you want them to rush to the library to check it out so they can find out what happens.
- Do not make the booktalk lengthy. Going on and on about the book is a sure way to make students lose interest in it.

Book Club

Thanks to that popular daytime talk show hostess, book clubs have become popular and fashionable. People have always enjoyed sharing and talking about books they are reading, and book club chatter comes naturally to most people. Take advantage of the popularity and organize some book clubs in your school. They are a great way to get people excited about reading. Discussing books with others takes literacy to a higher cognitive level for students as they ask questions, predict, compare and contrast, and make inferences. Here are some things to consider:

- When can you host the meeting(s)? Will it be before school ("Early Bird Book Club"), during school (consider a "Literacy Lunch"), or after hours?

- Will the book club be a program you offer alone as a library program or something you collaborate on with teachers or teaching teams, specialists, etc.?

- Who will participate? Is enrollment open to anyone interested, or will you choose a particular class, students who meet specific criteria, students recommended by their teachers, randomly chosen students, etc.?

- What book(s) will you choose? Check popular book lists and reviews and ask colleagues for recommendations. Try not to choose a book that most people have already read.

- Where will you get copies of the book for all participants? Are multiple copies already available to you, or will they need to be purchased by the school or from the library budget? What will happen to the books after the book club?

- How will you ensure good discussion? Have some conversation starters and topics ready in case the discussion is not free-flowing.

Another fun trend is to have a book club for adults in your building. Although some schools have book clubs that read professional teaching books, you might consider hosting one that reads a fiction bestseller. A faculty and staff book club allows staff members to interact with one another in a different way than they normally do; you can choose more complex books for this club than you would for a student book club. Some of these issues must be considered in this type of book club as well, but staff members can be required to purchase their own copies of the book. Also, enrollment is most often open, and meetings can take place outside of the school building or after the school day. Faculty/staff book clubs offer staff members the opportunity to develop or strengthen interpersonal relationships with coworkers while enjoying and discussing good literature in a comfortable environment.

Contests

Contests are a great way to get students into your library, where they might not be able to resist the allure of a good book. The purpose of contests is to get students excited about your library. Prizes can be purchased or obtained by donation. You might have to solicit for donations (see Figure 19-1 for a sample donation request letter), but local businesses will often be willing to give something to benefit children in a neighboring school. Make sure to vary the type of contest and the prizes so that students don't lose interest. Here are some contests you might try:

- Name that book: You give a line, summary, or character names, and students give you the title.

Figure 19-1. Sample Donation Request Letter

Dear Business Patron:

Killough Middle School, in an effort to promote literacy in students of our community, has a program titled **Charged Readers**; its motto is "Mission Possible: Get Charged with a Good Book." We know that strong readers are strong students who become the strong business leaders of tomorrow. Our program recognizes outstanding readers school-wide who read novels throughout the year and will (in May) be invited to attend a live auction; they will be given points that they can use to "bid" on prizes as a reward for their reading excellence. Thus far we have approximately 200 students eligible—that's exciting!

We ask for your help in this venture and invite you to participate by donating prizes or gift certificates for our auction. Your participation will send a strong and positive message to our students, staff, parents, and community members that you recognize the importance of education and literacy in today's world and in our students' futures.

We thank you in advance for your consideration of our request and for your help. If you would like more information on the program, please call us at . . .

Sincerely,

Marco Zannier, Librarian
Killough Middle School, Alief ISD

- -

Killough Middle School Representative: _____

Position: _____   Date: _____

Killough's Sales Tax Exemption #: _____

Reason for exemption: public school

- Trivia: Students must do research to find the answers.
- Art: Students design a book cover, movie poster, logo, etc.
- Writing: Students write a poem or news article based on a book.
- Reading incentive: This type of contest is based on reading (number of books, time spent reading, etc.). You must create some way for students to keep a log or records, and teachers or parents should verify that requirements were met.
- Scavenger hunt: Find items in the library or in books.

Special Events

If you are an event planner by nature, consider using your expertise to create events at your school that enhance instruction and promote the library. You could organize an Earth Day celebration with an "old book" swap, reading by sunlight, etc., a poetry slam, a "come as your favorite character" party, etc. These types of events get everyone involved in a fun way and help you connect to students and staff; they also promote you and your library. However, these are often massive undertakings for one person alone. Create a committee, use volunteers (if they are available), or convince some friendly coworkers to help you plan and share the workload. Make sure you consider budget from the start for refreshments, decorations, give-aways, etc. Advertise the event so you get plenty of participation. Make sure not to schedule concurrent projects so that you can devote enough time and resources to making the event successful. Take plenty of pictures. Photos can be posted in the library or on the library's Web site or used in a newsletter as publicity.

Bringing in Visitors

New faces with talents and knowledge that enhance instruction can get students excited about learning and can break the routine of "business as usual." Visitors offer new and interesting perspectives and they present educational information in a fun and engaging way. Some visitors you might schedule are:

- Authors—contact publishers and local bookstores, check for local authors who make school visits, and do some research to find out who the favorite authors are in your school
- Storytellers—online storyteller organizations can give you more information and put you in contact with storytellers who visit your area
- The youth librarian of your local public library
- Local singers, dancing troupes, acting groups, etc.
- Animal experts (from a local pet shop or zoo, for example) who might be able to bring in live specimens
- Guest speakers in different careers
- Firefighters—yes, they bring the truck!
- Dentists, to demonstrate the importance of dental hygiene
- Local artists who can bring in samples of their work
- A docent from a local museum

Visitors like these can expose children to experiences they may not otherwise have had. Their visits enrich your students' learning and allow them to explore and discover.

Be aware that some of these visits are free while others must be paid for (some authors charge $2,000 or more), so plan accordingly. Find out how many audience members the visitor will be comfortable with and schedule appropriately. Promote the event. Send the visitor a thank-you note. It is nice to include some photographs or something created or signed by those in attendance. Evaluate the program afterward using feedback from participants to decide if it was an effective and positive experience that was worth the effort, expense, time, etc. Keep a portfolio of visitors to help with future planning; this will also help you to make recommendations of visitors to other librarians or teachers.

Evaluation

Part V consists of just one chapter: Chapter 20, "Evaluating and Closing Out the Year." The school year may have ended but you are far from done. This final chapter will help you to evaluate both your library and yourself. How well did you perform your job? Did you meet your own expectations and the expectations or your school community? Were resources adequate for your library to meet the needs of your library users? Should more services be made available? This chapter will help you finish up the year, prepare for the next year, and improve library services to your school.

Evaluating and Closing Out the Year

Add an item on your calendar for the last week of school that reminds you to read this chapter again at that time.

Although this is the final chapter, you are by no means done. When the school year comes to a close, you will already be preparing for next year and everything that you will do even better than you did this year. You have learned so much and have worked hard to make yourself an asset to the staff and students; you have created and maintained a library that is a welcoming place full of amazing resources and wonderful programming. At the end of the year it will be time to reflect and get some data that you can use to help you plan for the year ahead.

Self-evaluation: The Basics

Take a look at some of the items discussed in Section I of this book and reflect on how you did this past year:

- Goals—Did you work on the goals you set for yourself? Did you accomplish any of them? Are there some that still need some work? Did some of the goals end up not being important or doable?

- Organization—How well did you stay organized? What techniques did you devise for staying organized? Do any changes need to be made to the system you have in place? Do you need to reevaluate how you schedule your time or library time? Does your office or the library need to be reorganized so it is more efficient or more pleasing?

- Communication—Did you use various techniques to communicate with your stakeholders so that they are aware of all the great things happening in your library? Did you try publishing a newsletter?

- Policies—Are the important policies in place? Do you have copies of important policies and documents posted?

IN THIS CHAPTER:

✔ Self-evaluation: The Basics

✔ Self-evaluation: The Roles of a Librarian

✔ Seeking Feedback from Others

✔ Final Reminders for the End of the Year

Self-evaluation: The Roles of a Librarian

Skim through Sections II through IV of this book and reflect on the various roles you play in the school. Were you a manager who utilized a balanced budget, maintained a useful and organized collection, and successfully supervised library personnel? Were you an information specialist who chose quality materials and helped your school community locate, access, and use all of the resources available to them? Were you a teacher and instructional specialist who got to know the school's curriculum and used programming, instruction, and collaboration with teachers to support and enrich that curriculum?

No one expected you to be Superman or Wonder Woman, so don't be hard on yourself. You probably did much better than you want to give yourself credit for. Your efforts contributed to the education and information literacy development of students in your school, and you worked with other educators in your building to make that happen. You also did a good job of learning about your faculty and students and how your library can better serve them. The library runs smoothly—for the most part—and you bought some pretty great materials for it that you have been promoting and using with students and teachers. Use the Self-evaluation Chart in Figure 20-1 to write down what you did well, what you need to work on, and how to improve in those areas.

Seeking Feedback from Others

Now that you have evaluated yourself, it is time to get a different perspective. Things you thought did not work well may have been huge hits with your school community of users, and things you felt were successes might be seen by them as areas for improvement. Ask the faculty and even students to help you improve your library and the services you offer by completing a

Figure 20-1. Self-evaluation Chart

	Things I did well	Things I need to do better	Strategies for improving
Librarian as **Library Administrator**			
Librarian as **Information Specialist**			
Librarian as **Teacher and Instructional Specialist**			

short survey about their experiences in your library this past year. Ask them to comment on important areas—the collection, collaboration, information-seeking assistance, etc.—and allow them to offer suggestions. The survey can be done on paper or electronically. Several services online allow you to create a survey and send the link out to all of your library users (see Figure 20-2). Once completed, the survey results are collected and tabulated for you, and reports can be printed for future reference.

Figure 20-2. Library User Online Survey

1. Please select closest job title: (Required)
   - ☐ Teacher
   - ☐ Paraprofessional
   - ☐ Specialist
   - ☐ Administrator
   - ☐ Counselor
   - ☐ Other non-teaching professional

2. How often have you visited or utilized the library and/or its services this past year? (If you choose "never," please select "n/a" on questions 3–5 below) (Required)
   - ☐ never
   - ☐ 1–5 times
   - ☐ 5–10 times
   - ☐ more than 10 times

3. What did you use the library for (check all that apply)? (Required)
   - ☐ checking out books, videos, equipment, etc.
   - ☐ bringing classes to use computers for research
   - ☐ bringing classes for reading or book check-out
   - ☐ collaborated with librarian for lesson planning, design, and implementation
   - ☐ hosting presentations (whether with students or adults/professionals)
   - ☐ hosting casual events
   - ☐ shopped in the café
   - ☐ "the Oasis" (Professional Room)
   - ☐ Other _____
   - ☐ n/a

4. Did you find the library easy to use/accessible/accommodating? (Required)
   - ☐ Yes
   - ☐ No
   - ☐ n/a

5. Did you find the library staff to be friendly and helpful? (Required)
   - ☐ Yes
   - ☐ No
   - ☐ n/a

(Cont'd.)

Figure 20-2. Library User Online Survey (Continued)

6. Were you aware that the library could provide help with locating resources beyond our collection and that the librarians can collaborate with you to design lessons, create online assignment Web pages, and co-teach research strategies and activities? *(Required)*

   ☐ Yes
   ☐ No

If you answered NO to question #6, skip ahead to #10 . . .

7. If you answered YES to question #6, have you ever collaborated with one of the librarians for a lesson?

   ☐ Yes
   ☐ No

8. If you HAVE collaborated, how would you rate your experience?

   ☐ It was successful and I enjoyed it - I will do it again.
   ☐ It was successful - but I probably won't do it again
   ☐ It was unsuccessful - but I'm willing to try again
   ☐ It was a bad experience - I will not be doing it again
   ☐ n/a

9. If you HAVE NOT collaborated, why not?

   ☐ I never had time
   ☐ There wasn't anywhere in my curriculum to "fit in" a collaborative lesson
   ☐ I didn't think librarians knew enough about my curriculum/teaching to be of help
   ☐ Just not interested
   ☐ Other _____
   ☐ n/a

10. If you answered NO to question #6, would you be interested in collaborating with the librarians next year?

    ☐ Yes
    ☐ No

11. Please give an overall rating of the libraries and the new librarians: (Required)

    ☐ poor
    ☐ fair
    ☐ good
    ☐ excellent

12. Please add comments/suggestions that will help us assess our first year and develop plans for next year (appreciated - not required):

    ```



    ```

    [Submit]

Use the results of your survey! Surveys are a wonderful tool for assessing whether or not you are meeting your users' needs and determining their attitudes toward your library program. Do not take results personally; think of evaluations as a way to allow your school community an opportunity to play a part in helping you do your job even better.

Final Reminders for the End of the Year

- Print out your budget spreadsheet and close out your "finances" binder; you might go ahead and make a new one for next year.

- Make sure you do not have (or know the status of and procedure for) any outstanding orders or delayed shipments.

- Create a file folder, paper or electronic, of all of your monthly reports from this past year.

- Add any items you weren't able to purchase to your "items to order" or "items for consideration" folder so you have them handy for your first order next year.

- File your inventory and withdrawn items reports.

- Be sure you have made arrangements for magazine and database subscription renewals so you do not have interruptions in service.

- Send a thank-you note to people who helped make your year easier or more successful, such as administrators, assistants, volunteers, and teachers who worked closely with you.

- Pack a few good books to read over summer vacation. If you don't have a book in your hands during all of that free time, how will you ever engage someone in a conversation about how awesome it is to be a school librarian?

Selected Policy Documents

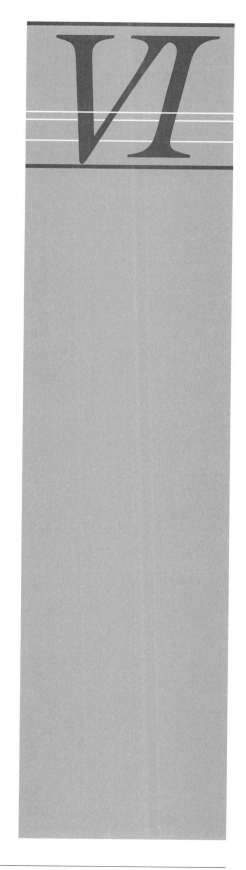

Part VI includes different policy documents: the Library Bill of Rights from the American Library Association along with two interpretations and two freedom statements, and a sample Acceptable Use Policies document along with a list of Web sites where other well-crafted AUPs can be found. Obviously, you will want to have many more policies available in your school library; these are provided as examples of the types of documents that you will need to collect or develop for your policy manual.

Library Bill of Rights, Interpretations, and Freedom Statements

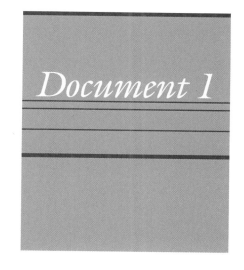

Document 1

Library Bill of Rights

The American Library Association affirms that all libraries are forums for information and ideas, and that the following basic policies should guide their services.

  I. Books and other library resources should be provided for the interest, information, and enlightenment of all people of the community the library serves. Materials should not be excluded because of the origin, background, or views of those contributing to their creation.

  II. Libraries should provide materials and information presenting all points of view on current and historical issues. Materials should not be proscribed or removed because of partisan or doctrinal disapproval.

  III. Libraries should challenge censorship in the fulfillment of their responsibility to provide information and enlightenment.

  IV. Libraries should cooperate with all persons and groups concerned with resisting abridgement of free expression and free access to ideas.

  V. A person's right to use a library should not be denied or abridged because of origin, age, background, or views.

  VI. Libraries which make exhibit spaces and meeting rooms available to the public they serve should make such facilities available on an equitable basis, regardless of the beliefs or affiliations of individuals or groups requesting their use.

Adopted June 18, 1948.

Amended February 2, 1961, and January 23, 1980; inclusion of "age" reaffirmed January 23, 1996, by the ALA Council.

Reprinted with permission of the American Library Association.

IN THIS DOCUMENT:

✔ Library Bill of Rights

✔ Interpretations

✔ Freedom Statements

Interpretations

Access to Resources and Services in the School Library Media Program: An Interpretation of the Library Bill of Rights

The school library media program plays a unique role in promoting intellectual freedom. It serves as a point of voluntary access to information and ideas and as a learning laboratory for students as they acquire critical thinking and problem solving skills needed in a pluralistic society. Although the educational level and program of the school necessarily shapes the resources and services of a school library media program, the principles of the Library Bill of Rights apply equally to all libraries, including school library media programs.

School library media professionals assume a leadership role in promoting the principles of intellectual freedom within the school by providing resources and services that create and sustain an atmosphere of free inquiry. School library media professionals work closely with teachers to integrate instructional activities in classroom units designed to equip students to locate, evaluate, and use a broad range of ideas effectively. Through resources, programming, and educational processes, students and teachers experience the free and robust debate characteristic of a democratic society.

School library media professionals cooperate with other individuals in building collections of resources appropriate to the developmental and maturity levels of students. These collections provide resources which support the curriculum and are consistent with the philosophy, goals, and objectives of the school district. Resources in school library media collections represent diverse points of view on current as well as historical issues.

While English is, by history and tradition, the customary language of the United States, the languages in use in any given community may vary. Schools serving communities in which other languages are used make efforts to accommodate the needs of students for whom English is a second language. To support these efforts, and to ensure equal access to resources and services, the school library media program provides resources which reflect the linguistic pluralism of the community.

Members of the school community involved in the collection development process employ educational criteria to select resources unfettered by their personal, political, social, or religious views. Students and educators served by the school library media program have access to resources and services free of constraints resulting from personal, partisan, or doctrinal disapproval. School library media professionals resist efforts by individuals or groups to define what is appropriate for all students or teachers to read, view, hear, or access via electronic means.

Major barriers between students and resources include but are not limited to: imposing age or grade level restrictions on the use of resources, limiting the use of interlibrary loan and access to electronic information, charging fees for information in specific formats, requiring permission from parents or teachers, establishing restricted shelves or closed collections, and labeling.

Policies, procedures, and rules related to the use of resources and services support free and open access to information.

The school board adopts policies that guarantee students access to a broad range of ideas. These include policies on collection development and procedures for the review of resources about which concerns have been raised. Such policies, developed by persons in the school community, provide for a timely and fair hearing and assure that procedures are applied equitably to all expressions of concern. School library media professionals implement district policies and procedures in the school.

Adopted July 2, 1986; amended January 10, 1990; July 12, 2000, by the ALA Council.
Reprinted with permission of the American Library Association.

Challenged Materials: An Interpretation of the Library Bill of Rights

The American Library Association declares as a matter of firm principle that it is the responsibility of every library to have a clearly defined materials selection policy in written form that reflects the Library Bill of Rights, and that is approved by the appropriate governing authority.

Challenged materials that meet the criteria for selection in the materials selection policy of the library should not be removed under any legal or extra-legal pressure. The Library Bill of Rights states in Article I that "Materials should not be excluded because of the origin, background, or views of those contributing to their creation," and in Article II, that "Materials should not be proscribed or removed because of partisan or doctrinal disapproval." Freedom of expression is protected by the Constitution of the United States, but constitutionally protected expression is often separated from unprotected expression only by a dim and uncertain line. The Constitution requires a procedure designed to focus searchingly on challenged expression before it can be suppressed. An adversary hearing is a part of this procedure.

Therefore, any attempt, be it legal or extra-legal, to regulate or suppress materials in libraries must be closely scrutinized to the end that protected expression is not abridged.

Adopted June 25, 1971; amended July 1, 1981; amended January 10, 1990, by the ALA Council.
Reprinted with permission of the American Library Association.

Freedom Statements

The Freedom to Read Statement

The freedom to read is essential to our democracy. It is continuously under attack. Private groups and public authorities in various parts of the country are working to remove or limit access to reading materials, to censor content in schools, to label "controversial" views, to distribute lists of "objectionable" books or authors, and to purge libraries. These actions apparently rise from a view that our national tradition of free expression is no longer valid; that censorship and suppression are needed to counter threats to safety or national security as well as to avoid the subversion of politics and the corruption of morals. We, as individuals devoted to reading and as librarians and publishers responsible for disseminating ideas, wish to assert the public interest in the preservation of the freedom to read.

Most attempts at suppression rest on a denial of the fundamental premise of democracy: that the ordinary individual, by exercising critical judgment, will select the good and reject the bad. We trust Americans to recognize propaganda and misinformation, and to make their own decisions about what they read and believe. We do not believe they are prepared to sacrifice their heritage of a free press in order to be "protected" against what others think may be bad for them. We believe they still favor free enterprise in ideas and expression.

These efforts at suppression are related to a larger pattern of pressures being brought against education, the press, art and images, films, broadcast media, and the Internet. The problem is not only one of actual censorship. The shadow of fear cast by these pressures leads, we suspect, to an even larger voluntary curtailment of expression by those who seek to avoid controversy or unwelcome scrutiny by government officials.

Such pressure toward conformity is perhaps natural to a time of accelerated change. And yet suppression is never more dangerous than in such a time of social tension. Freedom has given the United States the elasticity to endure strain. Freedom keeps open the path of novel and creative solutions, and enables change to come by choice. Every silencing of a heresy, every enforcement of an orthodoxy, diminishes the toughness and resilience of our society and leaves it less able to deal with controversy and difference.

Now as always in our history, reading is among our greatest freedoms. The freedom to read and write is almost the only means for making generally available ideas or manners of expression that can initially command only a small audience. The written word is the natural medium for the new idea and the untried voice from which come the original contributions to social growth. It is essential to the extended discussion that serious thought requires, and to the accumulation of knowledge and ideas into organized collections.

We believe that free communication is essential to the preservation of a free society and a creative culture. We believe that these pressures toward conformity present the danger of limiting the range and variety of inquiry and expression on which our democracy and our culture depend. We believe that every American community must jealously guard the freedom to publish and to circulate, in order to preserve its own freedom to read. We believe that publishers and librarians have a profound responsibility to give validity to that freedom to read by making it possible for the readers to choose freely from a variety of offerings. The freedom to read is guaranteed by the Constitution. Those with faith in free people will stand firm on these constitutional guarantees of essential rights and will exercise the responsibilities that accompany these rights.

We therefore affirm these propositions:

1. It is in the public interest for publishers and librarians to make available the widest diversity of views and expressions, including those that are unorthodox, unpopular, or considered dangerous by the majority.

   Creative thought is by definition new, and what is new is different. The bearer of every new thought is a rebel until that idea is refined and tested. Totalitarian systems attempt to maintain themselves in power by the ruthless suppression of any concept that challenges the established orthodoxy. The power of a democratic system to adapt to change is vastly strengthened by the freedom of its citizens to choose widely from among conflicting opinions offered freely to them. To stifle every nonconformist idea at birth would mark the end of the democratic process. Furthermore, only through the constant activity of weighing and selecting can the democratic mind attain the strength demanded by times like these. We need to know not only what we believe but why we believe it.

2. Publishers, librarians, and booksellers do not need to endorse every idea or presentation they make available. It would conflict with the public interest for them to establish their own political, moral, or aesthetic views as a standard for determining what should be published or circulated.

   Publishers and librarians serve the educational process by helping to make available knowledge and ideas required for the growth of the mind and the increase of learning. They do not foster education by imposing as mentors the patterns of their own thought. The people should have the freedom to read and consider a broader range of ideas than those that may be held by any single librarian or publisher or government or church. It is wrong that what one can read should be confined to what another thinks proper.

3. It is contrary to the public interest for publishers or librarians to bar access to writings on the basis of the personal history or political affiliations of the author.

   No art or literature can flourish if it is to be measured by the political views or private lives of its creators. No society of free people can flourish that draws up lists of writers to whom it will not listen, whatever they may have to say.

4. There is no place in our society for efforts to coerce the taste of others, to confine adults to the reading matter deemed suitable for adolescents, or to inhibit the efforts of writers to achieve artistic expression.

   To some, much of modern expression is shocking. But is not much of life itself shocking? We cut off literature at the source if we prevent writers from dealing with the stuff of life. Parents and teachers have a responsibility to prepare the young to meet the diversity of experiences in life to which they will be exposed, as they have a responsibility to help them learn to think critically for themselves. These are affirmative responsibilities, not to be discharged simply by preventing them from reading works for which they are not yet prepared. In these matters values differ, and values cannot be legislated; nor can machinery be devised that will suit the demands of one group without limiting the freedom of others.

5. It is not in the public interest to force a reader to accept the pre-judgment of a label characterizing any expression or its author as subversive or dangerous.

    The ideal of labeling presupposes the existence of individuals or groups with wisdom to determine by authority what is good or bad for others. It presupposes that individuals must be directed in making up their minds about the ideas they examine. But Americans do not need others to do their thinking for them.

6. It is the responsibility of publishers and librarians, as guardians of the people's freedom to read, to contest encroachments upon that freedom by individuals or groups seeking to impose their own standards or tastes upon the community at large; and by the government whenever it seeks to reduce or deny public access to public information.

    It is inevitable in the give and take of the democratic process that the political, the moral, or the aesthetic concepts of an individual or group will occasionally collide with those of another individual or group. In a free society individuals are free to determine for themselves what they wish to read, and each group is free to determine what it will recommend to its freely associated members. But no group has the right to take the law into its own hands and to impose its own concept of politics or morality upon other members of a democratic society. Freedom is no freedom if it is accorded only to the accepted and the inoffensive. Further, democratic societies are more safe, free, and creative when the free flow of public information is not restricted by governmental prerogative or self-censorship.

7. It is the responsibility of publishers and librarians to give full meaning to the freedom to read by providing books that enrich the quality and diversity of thought and expression. By the exercise of this affirmative responsibility, they can demonstrate that the answer to a "bad" book is a good one, the answer to a "bad" idea is a good one.

    The freedom to read is of little consequence when the reader cannot obtain matter fit for that reader's purpose. What is needed is not only the absence of restraint, but the positive provision of opportunity for the people to read the best that has been thought and said. Books are the major channel by which the intellectual inheritance is handed down, and the principal means of its testing and growth. The defense of the freedom to read requires of all publishers and librarians the utmost of their faculties, and deserves of all Americans the fullest of their support.

We state these propositions neither lightly nor as easy generalizations. We here stake out a lofty claim for the value of the written word. We do so because we believe that it is possessed of enormous variety and usefulness, worthy of cherishing and keeping free. We realize that the application of these propositions may mean the dissemination of ideas and manners of expression that are repugnant to many persons. We do not state these propositions in the comfortable belief that what people read is unimportant. We believe rather that what people read is deeply important, that ideas can be dangerous, but that the suppression of ideas is fatal to a democratic society. Freedom itself is a dangerous way of life, but it is ours.

This statement was originally issued in May of 1953 by the Westchester Conference of the American Library Association and the American Book Publishers Council, which in 1970 consolidated with the American Educational Publishers Institute to become the Association of American Publishers.

Adopted June 25, 1953; revised January 28, 1972, January 16, 1991, July 12, 2000, June 30, 2004, by the ALA Council and the AAP Freedom to Read Committee.

A Joint Statement by: American Library Association and Association of American Publishers.

Reprinted with permission of the American Library Association.

Freedom to View Statement

The FREEDOM TO VIEW, along with the freedom to speak, to hear, and to read, is protected by the First Amendment to the Constitution of the United States. In a free society, there is no place for censorship of any medium of expression. Therefore these principles are affirmed:

> To provide the broadest access to film, video, and other audiovisual materials because they are a means for the communication of ideas. Liberty of circulation is essential to insure the constitutional guarantee of freedom of expression.

> To protect the confidentiality of all individuals and institutions using film, video, and other audiovisual materials.

> To provide film, video, and other audiovisual materials which represent a diversity of views and expression. Selection of a work does not constitute or imply agreement with or approval of the content.

> To provide a diversity of viewpoints without the constraint of labeling or prejudging film, video, or other audiovisual materials on the basis of the moral, religious, or political beliefs of the producer or filmmaker or on the basis of controversial content.

> To contest vigorously, by all lawful means, every encroachment upon the public's freedom to view.

This statement was originally drafted by the Freedom to View Committee of the American Film and Video Association (formerly the Educational Film Library Association) and was adopted by the AFVA Board of Directors in February 1979. This statement was updated and approved by the AFVA Board of Directors in 1989.

Endorsed January 10, 1990, by the ALA Council.

Reprinted with permission of the American Library Association.

Acceptable Use Policies for Woodland School District Network (2022P)

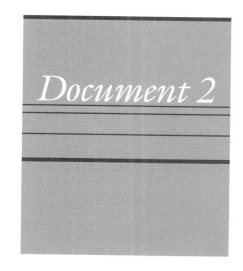

Document 2

These procedures are written to support the Electronic Resources Policy of the Board of Directors and to promote positive and effective digital citizenship among students and staff. Digital citizenship represents more than technology literacy. Successful, technologically fluent digital citizens live safely and civilly in an increasingly digital world. They recognize that information posted on the Internet is public and permanent and can have a long-term impact on an individual's life and career. Expectations for student and staff behavior online are no different than face-to-face interactions.

Network

The District network includes wired and wireless computers and peripheral equipment, files and storage, e-mail and Internet content (blogs, web sites, web mail, groups, wikis, etc.). The District reserves the right to prioritize the use of, and access to, the network.

All use of the network must support education and research and be consistent with the mission of the District.

Acceptable Network Use by District Students and Staff Includes:

- Creation of files, projects, videos, web pages and podcasts using network resources in support of educational research;

- Participation in blogs, wikis, bulletin boards, social networking sites and groups and the creation of content for podcasts, e-mail and web pages that support educational research;

- With parental permission, the online publication of original educational material, curriculum related materials and student work. Sources outside the classroom or school must be cited appropriately;

- Staff use of the network for incidental personal use in accordance with all District policies and guidelines;

IN THIS DOCUMENT:
- ✔ Network
- ✔ Internet Safety
- ✔ Copyright
- ✔ Network Security and Privacy
- ✔ Archive and Backup
- ✔ Disciplinary Action
- ✔ AUP Forms

- Connection of staff personal laptops to the district network after checking with (*insert title of position, i.e., technology director, IT director, assistant superintendent*) to confirm that the laptop is equipped with up-to-date virus software, compatible network card and is configured properly. Connection of any personal electronic device is subject to all guidelines in this document.

Unacceptable Network Use by District Students and Staff Includes but Is Not Limited to:

- Personal gain, commercial solicitation and compensation of any kind;
- Liability or cost incurred by the district;
- Downloading, installation and use of games, audio files, video files or other applications (including shareware or freeware) without permission or approval from the (*insert title of position*);
- Support or opposition for ballot measures, candidates and any other political activity;
- Hacking, cracking, vandalizing, the introduction of viruses, worms, Trojan horses, time bombs and changes to hardware, software and monitoring tools;
- Unauthorized access to other district computers, networks and information systems;
- Cyberbullying, hate mail, defamation, harassment of any kind, discriminatory jokes and remarks;
- Information posted, sent or stored online that could endanger others (e.g., bomb construction, drug manufacturing);
- Accessing, uploading, downloading, storage and distribution of obscene, pornographic or sexually explicit material; and
- Attaching unauthorized equipment to the district network. Any such equipment will be confiscated and destroyed.

The District will not be responsible for any damages suffered by any user, including but not limited to, loss of data resulting from delays, non-deliveries, mis-deliveries or service interruptions caused by its own negligence or any other errors or omissions. The District will not be responsible for unauthorized financial obligations resulting from the use of, or access to, the District's computer network or the Internet.

Internet Safety

Personal Information and Inappropriate Content:

- Students and staff should not reveal personal information, including a home address and phone number, on web sites, blogs, podcasts, videos, wikis, e-mail or as content on any other electronic medium.

Acceptable Use Policies for Woodland School District Network

- Students and staff should not reveal personal information about another individual on any electronic medium.

- No student pictures or names can be published on any class, school or District web site unless the appropriate permission has been verified according to district policy.

- If students encounter dangerous or inappropriate information or messages, they should notify the appropriate school authority.

Filtering and Monitoring

Filtering software is used to block or filter access to visual depictions that are obscene and all child pornography in accordance with the Children's Internet Protection Act (CIPA). Other objectionable material could be filtered. The determination of what constitutes "other objectionable" material is a local decision.

- Filtering software is not 100% effective. While filters make it more difficult for objectionable material to be received or accessed, filters are not a solution in themselves. Every user must take responsibility for his or her use of the network and Internet and avoid objectionable sites;

- Any attempts to defeat or bypass the District's Internet filter or conceal Internet activity are prohibited: proxies, https, special ports, modifications to district browser settings and any other techniques designed to evade filtering or enable the publication of inappropriate content;

- E-mail inconsistent with the educational and research mission of the District will be considered SPAM and blocked from entering District e-mail boxes;

- The District will provide appropriate adult supervision of Internet use. The first line of defense in controlling access by minors to inappropriate material on the Internet is deliberate and consistent monitoring of student access to District computers;

- Staff members who supervise students, control electronic equipment or have occasion to observe student use of said equipment online, must make a reasonable effort to monitor the use of this equipment to assure that student use conforms to the mission and goals of the District; and

- Staff must make a reasonable effort to become familiar with the Internet and to monitor, instruct and assist effectively.

Copyright

Downloading, copying, duplicating and distributing software, music, sound files, movies, images or other copyrighted materials without the specific written permission of the copyright owner is generally prohibited. However, the duplication and distribution of materials for educational purposes are

WEB SITES FOR ACCEPTABLE USE POLICIES

Adams Township School District
http://www.adams.k12.mi.us/2006-09%20Technology
%20Plan.htm

Addison Central School District
https://portal.addisoncsd.org/community/Public%20Forms/
District%20Plans/Technology%20Acceptable%20Use
%20Policy.pdf

Arlington Central School District
http://www.arlingtonschools.org/index.php?option=com_
content&task=view&id=198&Itemid=319

Barker Central School District
http://www.barkercsd.net/113210910103715990/lib/
113210910103715990/BCS_ELE_STU_AUA_08_09.pdf

Carbon School District
http://www.carbon.k12.ut.us/pdf_new/aup_staff_2008_
revision.pdf

Ceres Unified School District
http://www.ceres.k12.ca.us/cusdweb/information/
accptable-use-policy.htm

Clark Public School District
http://www.clarkschools.org/site_res_view_folder.aspx?id=
ae7856e1-07dd-42ca-98ea-01b2ed556874

Eagle County School District
http://eagleschools.net/departments/technology/forms/
15-ecsdacceptableuse.pdf

East Islip School District
http://www.eischools.org/www/eischools/site/hosting/
2007-2008/TechnologyPlanfinal.pdf

Easton Area School District
http://www.eastonsd.org/POLICIES/AUP2006.pdf

E.E. Smith Middle School
http://www.duplinschools.net/education/components/scrapbook/
default.php?sectiondetailid=10599&PHPSESSID=
87158e56839c46e38614c6685268023a

Evergreen School District
http://www.evergreen.k12.oh.us/forms/StaffAUP.pdf

Freedom Area School District
http://www.freedomschools.k12.wi.us/acceptableusepolicy.cfm

Genoa-Kingston Community Unit School District
http://gkschools.org/InternetPermission.pdf

Governor Wentworth Regional School District
http://www.govwentworth.k12.nh.us/district/acceptableuse.html

Green Island Union Free School District
http://www.greenisland.org/pdf/techplan/2007TechnologyPlan.pdf

Hampden-Wilbraham Regional School District
http://www.hwrsd.org/employees/forms/aup.pdf

Kentucky Department of Education
http://www.education.ky.gov/KDE/Administrative+Resources/
Technology/Additional+Technology+Resources/Acceptable+
Use+Policy+Guidelines+and+State+Requirements+for+
Student+and+Staff+Access+to+Electronic+I.htm

Liberty Central School District
http://www.libertyk12.org/central/tech/aup.pdf

Lockney ISD
http://www.lockney.isd.tenet.edu/TechPlan/aup.pdf

Martin County School District
http://www.sbmc.org/departments/et/_docs/2007-06-09-
Technology_Plan.pdf

Muscogee County School District
http://mcsdga.net/inside/technology/techplan/techplan06_
appb_aup_rev_07-05.pdf

Northwest Educational Technology Consortium
http://www.netc.org/planning/planning/aup.php

Philadelphia School District
http://www.phila.k12.pa.us/aup/aup_english.html

Plano I.S.D.
http://k-12.pisd.edu/aug.htm

Richardson ISD
http://libraries.risd.org/bhslib/downloads/AUP%20Document
.pdf

Sacramento City Unified School District
http://www.scusd.edu/education_technology/aup.htm

Santa Rosa School District
http://www.santarosa.k12.fl.us/pdc/docs/0809/63-11-31_
AUPEmployee08-09.pdf

School District of Shiocton
http://www.shiocton.k12.wi.us/tech_plan.cfm

Solana Beach School District
http://www.sbsd.k12.ca.us/district/technology/TUP07-12/
SolanaBeachTUP.pdf

St. Johns County School District
http://www.stjohns.k12.fl.us/rules/aup

Utica City School District
http://www.uticaschools.org/main/computeruse/
ComputerUsePolicy.pdf

Virginia Department of Education
http://www.doe.virginia.gov/VDOE/Technology/AUP/home.shtml

Woodland Public Schools
http://www.woodlandschools.org/index.php?q=node/578

Yorktown Central School District
http://www.yorktowncsd.org/docs/technology/technologyplan
.pdf

permitted when such duplication and distribution fall within the Fair Use Doctrine of the United States Copyright Law (Title 17, USC) and content is cited appropriately.

All student work is copyrighted. Permission to publish any student work requires permission from the parent or guardian.

Network Security and Privacy

Network Security

Passwords are the first level of security for a user account. System logins and accounts are to be used only by the authorized owner of the account for authorized district purposes. Students and staff are responsible for all activity on their account and must not share their account password.

The following procedures are designed to safeguard network user accounts:

- Change passwords according to district policy;
- Do not use another user's account;
- Do not insert passwords into e-mail or other communications;
- If you write down your user account password, keep it in a secure location;
- Do not store passwords in a file without encryption;
- Do not use the "remember password" feature of Internet browsers; and
- Lock the screen, or log off, if leaving the computer.

Student Data Is Confidential

District staff must maintain the confidentiality of student data in accordance with the Family Educational Rights and Privacy Act (FERPA).

No Expectation of Privacy

The District provides the network system, e-mail and Internet access as a tool for education and research in support of the District's mission. The District reserves the right to monitor, inspect, copy, review and store, without prior notice, information about the content and usage of:

- The network;
- User files and disk space utilization;
- User applications and bandwidth utilization;
- User document files, folders and electronic communications;
- E-mail;
- Internet access; and
- Any and all information transmitted or received in connection with network and e-mail use.

No student or staff user should have any expectation of privacy when using the district's network. The district reserves the right to disclose any electronic messages to law enforcement officials or third parties as appropriate. All documents are subject to the public records disclosure laws of the State of Washington.

Archive and Backup

Backup is made of all District e-mail correspondence for purposes of public disclosure and disaster recovery. Barring power outage or intermittent technical issues, staff and student files are backed up on district servers nightly—Monday through Friday. Refer to the District retention policy for specific records retention requirements.

Disciplinary Action

All users of the District's electronic resources are required to comply with the District's policy and procedures *[and agree to abide by the provisions set forth in the District's user agreement]*. Violation of any of the conditions of use explained in the (*District's user agreement*), Electronic Resources Policy or in these procedures could be cause for disciplinary action, including suspension or expulsion from school and suspension or revocation of network and computer access privileges.

Revision Date: 10/27/08

AUP Forms

Acceptable Use Policies (AUP) forms for staff, students and volunteers must be filled out **before** accessing network resources. By signing this form, you are declaring that all use of the system will be in support of education and research and consistent with the mission of the district.

Reprinted with permission from Michael Green, Woodland Public Schools.

Directory of Essential Sources and Suppliers for School Library Media Centers

Part VII provides a directory of essential sources and suppliers for your school library media center. This directory brings together extensive lists of resources that school library media specialists will use as a ready reference, almost on a daily basis. It consists of seven sections:

- Sources for book reviews: a list of sources to find book reviews, for use in collection development of book purchases.

- Sources for non-print reviews: a list of sources of non-print materials, for use in collection development of audiovisuals and other non-print materials.

- Book vendors: a list of major book distributors, for use in ordering books.

- Periodical vendors: a list of subscription services/journal jobbers for use in purchasing periodicals.

- Sources for purchasing equipment, furnishings, and suppliers: a list of companies that carry library supplies and furniture.

- Selected audiovisual producers and distributors: a list of companies that produce and sell audiovisuals.

- Filtering software packages: listing software that helps protect and filter information from the Internet.

Where possible, addresses, phone numbers, e-mail addresses, and/or URLs are listed to facilitate contacting the companies and sources listed in this directory.

Essential Sources for School Library Media Centers

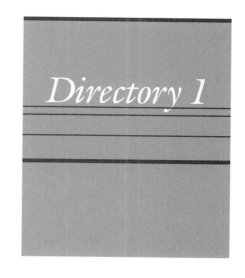

Directory 1

Sources for Book Reviews

ALAN Review
National Council of Teachers of English, Assembly on Literature for Adolescents, Digital Library & Archives, University Libraries. 1972. $20.00. 3/year.
Virginia Tech, Blacksburg, VA 24062-9001
www.alan-ya.org/the-alan-review/
http://scholar.lib.vt.edu/ejournals/ALAN/alan-review.html.
Editors: James Blasingame (James.Blasingame@asu.edu) and Lori A. Goodson (lagoodson@cox.net).

Book Review Digest Plus
H. W. Wilson
950 University Ave., Bronx, NY 10452
(718) 588-8400
(800) 367-6770
www.hwwilson.com/databases/brdig.htm

Bookbird
International Board of Books for Young People, Church of Ireland College of Education. 1963. 4/year.
96 Upper Rathmines Road, Dublin 6, Ireland
http://www.ibby.org/index.php?id=276
bookbirdvc@oldtown.ie

Booklist
American Library Association. 1905. $99.50. 22/year.
50 E. Huron St., Chicago, IL 60611
(800) 545-2433
http://www.ala.org/ala/booklist/booklist.cfm

Books in Canada
The Canadian Review of Books Ltd. 1971. In the United States: $58 for individuals, $72 for libraries and institutions. 9/year.

6021 Yonge St., Suite 1014, Toronto, Ontario, M2M 3W2, Canada
(416) 222-7139
Fax: (416) 222-9384
www.booksincanada.com
olga.stein@rogers.com

BooksInPrint.com
R. R. Bowker
630 Central Ave., New Providence, NJ 07974
(908) 286-1090
(888) 269-5372
www.booksinprint.com
orderinfo@bowker.com

Bulletin of the Center for Children's Books (formerly Center for Children's Books Bulletin)
Johns Hopkins University Press. 1947.
Print or online: $85. Print and online: $119. Print: $53. Students: $15. 12/year
2715 North Charles Street, Baltimore, MD 21218-4363
(800) 548-1784
Fax: (410) 516-6968
www.jhupress.edu/journals
jlorder@jhupress.edu

Canadian Children's Literature
Centre for Research in Young People's Text and Culture, University of Winnipeg. 1975.
Individuals, $50. Institutions, $75. Add $10 for shipping to the United States. 2/year.
3rd floor Centennial Hall, 515 Portage Ave., Winnipeg MB R3B 2E9
(204) 786-9351
Fax: (204) 774-4134
http://ccl.uwinnipeg.ca/
ccl@uwinnipeg.ca

CBC Features
Children's Book Council Inc.
As of Spring 2008, the publication is an e-newsletter only. One-time fee of $60. 2/year.
12 West 37th St., 2nd Floor, New York, NY 10018-7480
(212) 966-1990
(800) 999-2160
www.cbcbooks.org
cbcfeatures@cbcbooks.org

Children's Core Collection
H. W. Wilson. $195 for 4 years. 1/year, with supplements.
950 University Ave., Bronx, NY 10452
(718) 588-8400
(800) 367-6770
www.hwwilson.com/print/childcat.cfm

Children's Literature Review
Gale Research Inc.
(800) 877-4253
Fax: (877) 363-4253
www.gale.cengage.com

ChildrensBooksInPrint.com
R. R. Bowker
630 Central Ave., New Providence, NJ 07974
(908) 286-1090
(888) 269-5372
www.childrensbooksinprint.com

Choice
American Library Association, ACRL. $315. 12/year.
PO Box 141, Annapolis Junction, MD 20701
(240) 646-7027
Fax: (301) 206-9789
www.ala.org/ala/acrl/acrlpubs/choice/home.cfm
choicesubscriptions@brightkey.net

CM: Canadian Review of Materials (formerly *CM: A Reviewing Journal of Canadian Materials for Young People*)
Manitoba Library Association. 22 issues (September to June).
167 Houde Drive, Winnipeg MB R3V 1C6
cm@umanitoba.ca

Horn Book Magazine
Horn Book Inc. 1924. 6/year.
56 Roland Street, Suite 200, Boston, MA 02129
(617) 628-0225
(800) 325-1170
Fax: (617) 628-0882
www.hbook.com
info@hbook.com

Instructor
Scholastic Inc. $8. 8/year. $14.95 for 16 issues.
557 Broadway, New York, NY 10012
(212) 343-6100
(866) 436-2455
www.scholastic.com/instructor

Kliatt (formerly *Kliatt Young Adult Paperback Book Guide*)
HighBeam Research. Strictly an online tool.
www.highbeam.com/Kliatt/publications.aspx

Library Journal
Reed Business Information. $150/20 issues. 6/year.
360 Park Avenue South, New York, NY 10010
(646) 746-6758
Fax: (646) 746-6631
www.libraryjournal.com

Library Media Connection (the merging of *Book Report, Library Talk,* and *Technology Connection*)
Linworth Publishing Inc. $69. 12/year.
3650 Olentangy River Rd., Suite 250, Columbus, OH 43214
(800) 786-5017
www.linworth.com/lmc/

Middle and Junior High School Core Collection
H. W. Wilson. $290/4 years of print edition.
Available in online and print formats.
University Ave., Bronx, NY 10452
(718) 588-8400
(800) 367-6770
www.hwwilson.com/print/mjhscat.cfm

Publisher's Weekly
Reed Elsevier Inc., Reed Business Information. $240. Weekly.
Available online and in print.
60 Park Avenue South, New York, NY 10010
(646) 746-6758
Fax: (646) 746-6631
www.publishersweekly.com

Quill and Quire
St. Joseph's Media Inc. 1935. $95/year. 10/year.
www.quillandquire.com

School Library Journal
$130/year. 12/year.
Available online and in print.
www.schoollibraryjournal.com

School Library Media Research
American Library Association
50 E. Huron St., Chicago, IL 60611
(800) 545-2433
www.ala.org

Senior High Core Collection
H. W. Wilson. $245/4 years of print edition.
Available in online and print formats.
University Ave., Bronx, NY 10452
(718) 588-8400
(800) 367-6770
www.hwwilson.com/Print/srhscat.cfm

Subject Guide to Children's Books in Print
R. R. Bowker.
630 Central Ave., New Providence, NJ 07974
(908) 286-1090
(888) 269-5372
www.bowker.co.uk/catalog/000051.htm

United States Board on Books for Young People Newsletter
United States Board on Books for Young People Inc. 1976. 2/year.
800 Barksdale Rd,. Newark, DE 19714-8139
www.usbby.org
usbby@reading.org

Voice of Youth Advocates
Scarecrow Press Inc. $34.95 for individuals. $40 for institutions. 6/year.
4501 Forbes Blvd., Suite 200, Lanham, MD 20706
(800) 233-1687
Fax: (717) 794-3852
www.voya.com
journals@rowman.com

Sources for Non-print Reviews

Booklist
American Library Association. 1905. $99.50. 22/year.
50 E. Huron St., Chicago, IL 60611
(800) 545-2433
www.ala.org/ala/booklist/booklist.cfm

Children and Libraries: The Journal of the Association for Library Service to Children (formerly Journal of Youth Services in Libraries)
Association of Library Service to Children, division of American Libraries Association. 2003. Nonmembers: $40. Journal is perquisite for members of ALSC.
50 E. Huron St., Chicago, IL 60611
(800) 545-2433
subscriptions@ala.org
www.ala.org/alsc

Children's Media Market Place, 3rd edition
Neal-Schuman Publishers Inc.
100 William St., Suite 2004, New York, NY 10038
(212) 925-8650
Fax: (212) 219-8916
www.neal-schuman.com

Classroom Computer Learning
Peter Li Inc.
2621 Dryden Rd., Suite 300, Dayton, OH 45439
(937) 298-8965
(800) 523-4625
Fax: (800) 370-4450
www.peterli.com

Curriculum Review
Curriculum Advisory Service
212 W. Superior Street, Suite 200, Chicago, IL 60610-3533
(312) 335-0037

Educational Film & Video Locator, 4th edition
R. R. Bowker. 1990–1991.
630 Central Ave., New Providence, NJ 07974
(908) 286-1090
(888) 269-5372
www.bowker.com

Educational Software Selector
Educational Products Information Exchange Institute. Individual site licenses: $79.95. Semiannual updates: $29.95.
103 Montauk Highway, Hampton Bays, NY 11946
(516) 728-9100
Fax: (516) 728-9228
www.epie.org
info@epie.org

Film & Video Finder Online
Access Innovations Inc.
PO Box 8640, Albuquerque, NM 87918
(800) 926-8328
www.nicem.com

School Library Journal
Reed Business Information, a division of Reed Elsevier Inc. $129.99. 12/year.
360 Park Avenue South, New York, NY 10010
(646) 746-6759
Fax: (646) 746-6689
www.schoollibraryjournal.com
slj@reedbusiness.com

Science Books & Films
American Association for the Advancement of Science. 1965. $45. 6/year.
1200 New York Ave. NW, Washington, DC 20005
(202) 326-6670
Fax: (202) 371-9849
www.sbfonline.com
sb&f@aaas.org

Essential Suppliers for School Library Media Centers

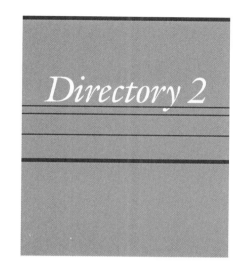

Directory 2

Book Vendors

Astran Inc.
Wholesale books in Spanish
6995 NW 82nd Ave., Miami, FL 33166
(305) 597-0064

Baker & Taylor Inc.
2550 West Tyvola Rd., Suite 300, Charlotte, NC 28217
(704) 998-3100
(800) 775-1800
www.btol.com
btinfo@btol.com

Bernan Associates
Government documents
4611-F Assembly Drive, Lanham, MD 20706-4391
(301) 459-2255
(800) 416-4385
Fax: (301) 459-0839
www.bernan.com

Blackwell Book Services
Beaver House Hythe Bridge St., Oxford, UK OX1 2ET
+44(0) 1865-333000
Fax: +44(0) 1865-791438
www.blackwell.com
sales@blackwell.co.uk

Book House Inc.
208 W. Chicago St., Jonesville, MI 49250
(800) 248-1146
Fax: (800) 858-9716
www.thebookhouse.com

IN THIS DIRECTORY:

✔ Book Vendors

✔ Periodical Vendors

✔ Sources for Purchasing Equipment, Furniture, and Supplies

✔ Selected AV Producers and Distributors

Book Wholesalers Inc.
1847 Mercer Rd., Lexington, KY 40511
(859) 231-9789
Fax: (859) 225-6700
www.bwibooks.com

Bookmen Inc.
525 N. 3rd St., Minneapolis, MN 55401
(612) 341-3333
Fax: (800) 266-5636
www.bookmen.com

The Booksource Inc.
1230 Macklind Ave., St. Louis, MO 63110
(314) 647-0600
(800) 444-0435
Fax: (314) 647-6850; (800) 647-1923
www.booksource.com

Bound to Stay Bound Books Inc.
1880 W. Morton Ave., Jacksonville, IL 62650
800-637-6586
Fax: (800) 747-2872
www.btsb.com
btsb@btsb.com

Brodart Co.
500 Arch Street, Williamsport, PA 17701
www.brodart.com
   Automation division
   (800) 474-9802 ext. 6772
   Fax: (800) 999-67799
   salesmkt@brodart.com
   Book services division
   (800) 233-8467
   (570) 326-2461
   Fax: (570) 326-2461
   bookinfo@brodart.com

Eastern Book Co.
55 Bradley Dr., Westbrook, ME 04092
(800) 937-0331
Fax: (800) 214-3895
www.ebc.com

Econo-Clad Books
PO Box 1777, Topeka, KS 66601
(800) 255-3205
Fax: (800) 628-2410

Emery-Pratt
1966 W. Main St., Owosso, MI 48867-1397
(989) 723-5291

(800) 248-3887
Fax: (800) 523-6379
www.emery-pratt.com

Follett Library Book Co.
4506 Northwest Hwy., Crystal Lake, IL 60014-7393
(800) 435-6170
Fax: (800) 852-5458
www.follett.com
customerservice@flr.follett.com

H. W. Wilson
Indexes and reference materials
950 University Ave., Bronx, NY 10452
(718) 588-8400
(800) 367-6770
www.hwwilson.com

Hispanic Book Distributors Inc.
1665 W. Grand Rd., Tucson, AZ 85745
(520) 882-9484
Fax: (520) 882-7696

Ingram Library Services
One Ingram Blvd., La Vergne, TN 37086
(800) 937-5300.
www.ingramlibrary.com
customer.requirements@ingrambook.com

International Book Centre
Foreign language books (ESL), children's, elementary materials
2007 Laurel Dr., Troy, MI 48085
(248) 879-8436
www.ibcbooks.com
ibc@ibcbooks.com

James Bennett Library Services
Australia and South Pacific titles
3 Narabang Way, Belrose NSW 2085, Australia
+612-9986-7000
Fax: +612-9986-7031
www.bennett.com

Lindsay & Howes Booksellers
Books from Great Britain
Littlemere, Petworth Rd., Wormley, Godalming, Surrey England GU8 5TU
44-428-684550
Fax: 44-01428-685542
books@lindhow.demon.co.uk

Midwest Library Services
11443 St. Charles Rock River, Bridgeton, MO 63044-2789
(314) 656-3201

(800) 325-8833
Fax: (314)739-1326; (800) 962-1009
www.midwestls.com

Nedbook International
PO Box 37600, 1030 BA Amsterdam, the Netherlands
31-20-6321771
Fax: 31-20-6340963
www.nedbook.nl
info@nedbook.nl

Perma-Bound
617 E. Vandalia Rd., Jacksonville, IL 62650
(217) 243-5451
(800) 637-6581
Fax: (217) 243-7505; (800) 551-1169
www.perma-bound.com
books@perma-bound.com

Puvill Libros
Books from Spain and Mexico
One East Park Dr., Paterson, NJ 07504
(973) 279-9054
Fax: (973) 278-1448
www.puvill.com
drorpuvill@aol.com

R. R. Bowker
630 Central Ave., New Providence, NJ 07974
(908) 286-1090
(888) 269-5372
www.bowker.com

Scholarly Book Center
451 Greenwich St., New York, NY 10013

YBP Library Services
999 Maple St., Contoocock, NH 03229
(603) 746-3102
(800) 258-3774
Fax: (603) 746-5628
www.ybp.com
ybplibraryservices@ybp.com

Periodical Vendors

B. H. Blackwell, Ltd.
British and European titles
Beaver House Hythe Bridge St., Oxford, UK OX1 2ET
44 (0) 1865-333000
www.blackwell.com

U.S. address
6024 Jean Road Building G, Lake Oswego, Oregon 97035
(800) 547-6426

EBSCO Information Services
110 Olmsted Street, Suite 100, Birmingham, AL 35242
(800) 815-9627
www.ebscobooks.com
    EBSCO Subscription Services–Midwest
    1140 Silver Lake Rd., Cary, IL 60013-1685
    (847) 639-2899

EVA Subscription Services
56 Maple Ave., PO Box 338, Shrewsbury, MA 01545
(800) 842-2077
www.evasub.com

Facts On File News Services
132 West 31st Street, 17th Floor, New York, NY 10001
(800) 322-8755
www.factsonfile.com

G. H. Arrow Co.
2066 West Hunting Park Ave., Philadelphia, PA 19140
(800) 775-ARROW
www.gharrow.com

Gale Cengage Learning
27500 Drake Road, Farmington Hills, MI 48331
(800) 877-4253
www.gale.cengage.com

Hawkeye Ink Back Issue Periodicals
Single back issue specialists
17435 Plainview Ave., PO Box 231, Redfield, SD 57469-0231
(605) 472-1559

The Haworth Press Inc., Taylor and Francis Group, LLC
325 Chestnut St., Suite 800, Philadelphia, PA 19106
(800) 354-1420
www.haworthpress.com

NewsBank Inc.
4501 Tamiami Trail North, Suite 316, Naples, FL 34103
(800) 762-8182
www.newsbank.com

Periodicals Service Co.
11 Main St., Germantown, NY 12526
(518) 537-4700
www.periodicals.com

ProQuest Information and Learning
789 E. Eisenhower Parkway, PO Box 1346, Ann Arbor, MI 48106-1346

(800) 521-0600

www.proquest.com

Research Periodicals and Book Services Inc.
PO Box 720728, Houston, TX 77272
(800) 521-0061
www.rpbs.com

Sage Publications
2455 Teller Road, Thousand Oaks, CA 91320
(805) 499-0721
www.sagepub.com

Swets Information Services
Hereweg 347B, 2161 CA Lisse, PO Box 800, 2160 SZ Lisse, the Netherlands
31-252-43-51-11
www.swets.com
> *U.S. address*
> 160 Ninth Avenue, PO Box 1459 Runnemede, NJ 08078
> (800) 645-6595

United States Book Exchange
Back issue periodicals
2969 West 25th Street, Cleveland, OH 44113
(216) 241-6960
www.usbe.com

W. T. Cox Subscriptions Inc.
201 Village Rd., Shallotte, NC 28470
(800) 571-9554.
www.wtcox.com

Sources for Purchasing Equipment, Furnishings, and Supplies

Advertising Specialties Inc.
160 W. Camino Real # 245, Boca Raton, FL 33432
(877) 274-6684
www.adspecialtiesinc.com

American Seating Co.
401 American Seating Center, Grand Rapids, MI 49504-4499
(600) 748-0268
www.americanseating.com

Bowker
Reference and reporting products and services.
630 Central Avenue, New Providence, NJ 07974.
(888) 269-5372
www.bowker.com

Bretford Manufacturing Inc.
11000 Seymour Avenue, Franklin Park, IL 60131
(800) 521-9614
www.bretford.com

Brodart Library Supplies and Furnishings
100 North Road, Clinton County Industrial Park, McElhattan, PA 17748-0280
(888) 820-4377
www.brodart.com

CBA
Furniture and shelving
PO Box 190728, Atlanta, GA 31119-0728
(800) 557-4222
www.cbaatlanta.com

Children's Book Council
Promotional supplies
12 W. 37th St., 2nd Floor, New York, NY 10018-7480
(212) 966-1990
www.cbcbooks.org

DEMCO Inc.
Library supplies and furniture
PO Box 7488, Madison, WI 53707
(800) 962-4463
www.demco.com

Fetzer Architectural Woodwork
6223 West Double Eagle Circle, Salt Lake City, UT 84118-8401
(801) 484-6103
www.fetzerwood.com

Fleetwood Group, Inc., Furniture Division
PO Box 1259, Holland, MI 49422-1259
(800) 257-6390
www.fleetwoodgroup.com

Follett Library Resources
1340 Ridgeview Drive, McHenry, IL 60050
(888) 511-5114
www.titlewave.com

Gaylord Bros.
Library supplies and furniture
PO Box 4901, Syracuse, NY 13221-4901
(800) 962-9580
www.gaylordmart.com

Grafco Inc.
Computer furniture
PO Box 71, Catasauqua, PA 18032
(800) 367-6169
www.grafco.com

Gressco Ltd.
Library furniture
328 Moravian Valley Road, Waunakee, WI 53597
(800) 345-3480
www.gresscoltd.com

Highsmith Company
Library and school products
W5227 State Road 106, Fort Atkinson, WI 53538
(800) 558-2110
www.highsmith.com

Infinite Furniture Solutions
1205 Industrial Blvd., Cameron, TX 76520
(877) 437-8880
www.infinitefurnituresolutions.com

International Library Furniture Co. Inc.
525 S. College, Keene, TX 76059
(817) 645-7750
www.internationallibrary.com

J. P. Jay and Associates Inc.
Library furniture
1313 Roth Ave., Allentown, PA 18102
(610) 435-9666
www.jpjay.com

Jasper Group, Library and Institutional Furnishings
694 N. Main Street, Troutman, NC 28166
(888) 440-8205
www.blantonandmoore.com

JD Pacific Rim Inc.
Fixtures and displays
4850 Gregg Rd., Pico Rivera, CA 90660
(888) 355-8889
http://store.jdpacificrim.com

Jim Quinn and Associates
Library furniture
PO Box 641, Altamont, NY 12009
(518) 861-7125
http://jimquinn.com

Kapco Library Products
1000 Cherry St., Kent, OH 44240
(800) 843-5368
www.kapcolibrary.com

Kurtz Bros.
School supplies, equipment, and furniture
400 Reed St., PO Box 393, Clearfield, PA 16830

(800) 252-3811

www.kurtzbros.com

Library Bureau

172 Industrial Road, Fitchburg, MA 01420

(800) 221-6638

www.librarybureau.com

Library Display Design Systems

PO Box 8143, Berlin, CT 06037

(860) 828-6069

www.librarydisplay.com

Library Store Inc.

Library supplies

112 E. South St., Tremont, IL 61568

(800) 548-7204

www.librarystore.com

Library Suppliers.com, an Online Division of University Products

(800) 628-1912

www.librarysuppliers.com

Mohawk Library Furniture

1609 Sherman Ave., Suite 312, Evanston, IL 60201

(647) 570-0448

www.mohawkfurniture.us

Montel High Density Storage Systems

225 4e Avenue, Montmagny, QC G5V 3S5, Canada

(418) 248-0235

(800) 772-7562 (U.S.)

www.montel.com

Neschen Americas

7091 Troy Hill Drive, Elkridge, MD 21075

(800) 257-7325

www.neschenusa.com

Newood Display Fixture Mfg. Co.

2125 Cross St., Eugene, OR 97402

(800) 233-9663

www.newood.com

Palmieri Furniture Ltd.

Library furniture and shelving

1230 Reid, Richmond Hill, ON L4B 1C4, Canada

(800) 413-4440

www.palmierifurniture.com

Pyramid School Products

School and art supplies

6510 North 54th St., Tampa, FL 33610

(800) 792-2644

www.pyramidsp.com

Ramsey Woodworks
214 Shelby Lane Ste G&F, Austin, TX 78745
(512) 773-0443
www.ramseyfurniture.com

Sauder Manufacturing Co.
School furniture
930 West Barre Rd., Archbold, OH 43502
(800) 537-1530
www.saudermfg.com

School Specialty
W6316 Design Drive, Greenville, WI 54942
(888) 388-3224
www.schoolspecialty.com

Scott Machine Development Corp.
Signage and engraving machines
200 Prospect Avenue, PO Box 88, Walton, NY 13858
(607) 865-6511
www.scottmachine.com

SICO America Inc.
Furniture
7525 Cahill Road, Minneapolis, MN 55439
(800) 328-6138
www.sicoinc.com

Spacesaver Corp.
Mobile storage and shelving systems
1450 Janesville Avenue, Fort Atkinson, WI 53538
(800) 492-3434
www.spacesaver.com

Stumps Prom
Party supplies
One Party Place, PO Box 305, South Whitley, IN 46787
(800) 348-5084
www.stumpsprom.com

Universal Air Lift Inc.
28010 NW 142nd Avenue, High Springs, FL 32643
(866) 526-3688
www.universalairlift.com

Vernon Library Supplies Inc.
2851 Cole Court, Norcross, GA 30071
(800) 878-0253
www.vernlib.com

Worden Co.
School and library furniture
199 E. 17th Street, Holland, MI 49423

(800) 748-0561
www.wordencompany.com

Selected AV Producers and Distributors

Comex Systems Inc.
Educational study guides, DVDs, and videotapes
5 Cold Hill Rd., Suite 24, Mendham, NJ 07945
(973) 543-2862
(800) 543-6959
Fax: (973) 543-9644
www.comexsystems.com

Coronet/MT Film & Video Inc.
108 Wilmot Rd., Deerfield, IL 60015
(708) 940-1260
(800) 621-2131
Fax: (708) 940-3600

Disney Educational Productions
105 Terry Dr., Suite 120, Newtown, PA 18940
(800) 295-5010
Fax: (215) 579-8589
http://dep.disney.go.com/educational/index

Encyclopedia Britannica Educational Corp
310 S. Michigan Ave., Chicago, IL 60604
(312) 347-7000
(800) 554-9862

Films for the Humanities and Sciences
PO Box 2053, Princeton, NJ 08543
(800) 257-5126
Fax: (609) 671-0266
www.films.com
custserv@films.com

Guidance Associates
31 Pineview Rd., Mt. Kisco, NY 10549
(941) 666-4100

Listening Library Inc.
1 Park Ave., Old Greenwich, CT 06870
(800) 243-4504
Fax: (800) 454-0606
www.listeninglibrary.com

Live Oak Media
PO Box 652, Pine Plains, NY 12567
(800) 788-1121
Fax: (866) 398-1070
www.liveoakmedia.com
info@liveoakmedia.com

FILTERING SOFTWARE PACKAGES

Barracuda Web Filter
(408) 342-5400
www.barracudanetworks.com

Bsafe Online
(850) 362-4310
www.bsafehome.com

Centipede Filter Pak
(866) 743-5196
www.centipedenetworks.com

CleanInternet
(866) 752-5326
www.cleaninternet.com

Cyber Patrol
(646) 789-4433
www.cyberpatrol.com

Cyber Snoop
(800) 732-7596
www.pearlsw.com

CyberSitter
www.solidoak.com

Cyblock Proxy
(877) 442-9346
www.wavecrest.net

Elron Internet Manager
(800) 393-1068
www.lansafe.com

I-Guard Content Filtering
(888) 999-3245
www.egl.net/iguard

Internet Filtering 8e6 Technologies
(888) 786-7999
www.8e6.com

Net Nanny
(866) 765-7233
www.netnanny.com

safeeyes
(877) 944-8080
www.internetsafety.com

SmartFilter
(800) 379-4944
www.securecomputing.com

WebSENSE Inc.
(800) 723-1166
www.websense.com

WebWatcher
(800) 340-6867
www.webwatchernow.com

Meridian Education Corp.
236 E. Front St., Bloomington, IL 61701
(309) 827-5455
(800) 727-5507
Fax: (309) 829-8621

PBS Video
1320 Braddock Place, Alexandria, VA 22314

Phoenix Films Inc
468 Park Avenue South, New York, NY 10016

Professional Media Service Corp
19122 S. Vermont Ave., Gardena, CA 90248
(800) 223-7672

Sesame Workshop (formerly Children's Television Workshop)
1 Lincoln Plaza, New York, NY 10023
(212) 595-3456
Fax: (212) 875-6088
www.sesameworkshop.org

Sign Media Inc.
4020 Blackburn Lane, Burtonsville, MD 20866
(301) 421-0268
(800) 475-4756
Fax: (301) 421-0270
www.signmedia.com
info@signmedia.com

Valley Record Distributors
1280 Santa Anita Court, Woodland, CA 95776
(530) 661-6600
Fax: (800) 999-1794
www.valley-media.com

Weston Woods Institute Inc.
389 Newton Turnpike, Weston CT 06883
(203) 222-8000

Index

Page numbers followed by the letter "f" indicate figures.